Sunset Ideas for
Recreation
Rooms

By the Editors of Sunset Books and Sunset Magazine

Lane Books · Menlo Park, California

Edited by Sherry Gellner

PHOTOGRAPHERS

Cover photograph: **Robert Cox. Armstrong Cork Company:** pages 88, 90. **Morley Baer:** page 54. **Jeremiah O. Bragstad:** pages 38, 39. **Ernest Braun:** pages 7 (bottom right), 36, 37, 50 (bottom). **Clyde Childress:** pages 41 (bottom), 66. **Glenn M. Christiansen:** page 72. **Robert C. Cleveland:** pages 12, 13. **Dearborn-Massar:** pages 50 (top), 52 (left), 56 (bottom). **Phil Fein & Associates:** page 47 (bottom right). **Richard Fish:** pages 8, 9, 16, 17 (top, bottom right), 22, 23 (bottom), 27, 31, 32, 33, 34, 40 (bottom), 41 (top), 43, 46, 47 (top right, bottom left), 48 (bottom), 51, 53 (top left, bottom), 58 (top), 60 (top left), 63, 80. **Frank L. Gaynor:** pages 47 (top left), 57 (bottom). **Bruce Harlow:** page 52 (top right). **Dean D. Hesketh Photography:** page 82. **Edmund Y. Lee:** pages 26, 44. **Leland Y. Lee:** pages 77, 79 (top). **Jack McDowell:** pages 6, 7 (top, bottom left), 10, 11, 14, 15, 20, 21, 67, 68, 69. **Nelson/Zellers Photo:** pages 5, 24. **Don Normark:** pages 18, 19, 25, 28, 29, 35, 40 (top), 42 (bottom), 60 (top right), 78, 84. **Georgia Pacific:** page 95 (top right). **Photographic Illustrators:** page 53 (top right). **Marvin Rand:** pages 59 (top), 60 (bottom right). **Martha Rosman:** pages 52 (bottom right), 56 (top), 57 (top), 62, 74 (top). **Douglas M. Simmonds:** page 81. **Werner Stoy:** page 49 (top). **Roger Sturtevant:** page 75. **Darrow M. Watt:** pages 30, 42 (top), 45, 48 (top), 55, 58 (bottom), 59 (bottom), 60 (bottom left), 70, 71, 74 (bottom), 79 (bottom), 83, 85, 86, 87, 92, 95 (top left), 96. **R. Wenkam:** pages 49 (bottom), 61, 65. **Steven Wilson:** page 64.

Executive Editor, Sunset Books: David E. Clark

Ninth Printing October 1973

Contents

Foreword

To each and every individual, the term "recreation" takes on a different meaning. To some, recreation is an exciting game of ping-pong or darts. To others, it is having an informal get-together, or simply enjoying an evening of television. To still others, it is pursuing a hobby. With this great diversity in mind, the editors of *Sunset* have compiled a book of ideas and suggestions for creating recreation centers covering a wide range of interests.

Since each home is a personal thing, bearing the stamp of the occupants, the recreation areas shown represent a great variety in style, design, and use. In the many rooms illustrated there is a wealth of ideas that you can use directly or adapt. Hopefully, there are answers for every family and for any need.

The book is divided into seven chapters:

- Game and party rooms
- Family rooms
- Sewing centers
- Home offices
- Studios and workshops
- Dens and studies
- How-to-do-it ideas

In each chapter there are suggestions for remodeling, for new additions, for converting garages into family centers (*Note:* Be sure to check local building codes), for storage, and for organizing the clutter of family living and play.

The last chapter is directed to the do-it-yourselfer. There are ideas for suspended ceiling installations, wall coverings, floor coverings, and painting — invaluable help in finishing a room or special area. Even if you do not intend to do the work yourself, you'll find help in making decisions as to types of materials to suit your particular situation.

GAME & PARTY ROOMS
...for fun and recreation

(See coverage of this room on page 24)

Pool table *stands next to ping-pong table in center of room. Cue rack is attached to wall behind with score-keeping device directly above. Raised hearth provides extra seating. Note stereo speaker in wall.*

A pavilion reserved for recreation

As the aerial photo shows, this house is made up of six pavilions—a building concept particularly suited to an active family of six who enjoy a wide variety of sport activities and like to entertain at home.

Sliding glass doors open two walls of the recreation pavilion (one to the pool, the other to an enclosed courtyard), increasing the size of the area when needed; with the doors closed, the room is an inviting retreat for smaller groups. The third wall contains a refreshment center, a large storage closet, and access to the hallway. The fourth wall has a brick fireplace and built-in seating with storage underneath. The re-sawn redwood interior adds extra warmth.

A double-paneled skylight in the center of the peaked roof, and clerestory windows above each wall, bathe the room with natural light by day; soffit lighting below the clerestory windows is used at night.

The entire house is linked by a stereo system, which provides dance music in the recreation area.

Architects: Fisher-Friedman Associates.

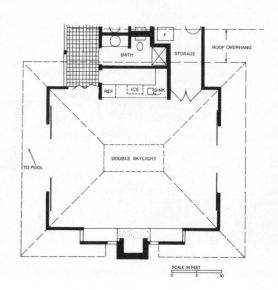

Refreshment center *contains small refrigerator, separate ice maker, and sink. Entrance is from hallway at left; storage closet is at right.*

Sliding glass doors *open wall and extend recreation area to poolside.*

Drawers *for games and equipment pull out below built-in seating; storage area for wood is under fireplace.*

Aerial photo *shows cluster of six pavilions. Recreation pavilion (lower right) is one with a double skylight.*

Storage wall *and louver windows fill former garage door opening. Cabinets are deep enough to hold extra chair and stereo system (note twin speakers above). Fully carpeted floor helps to reduce noise.*

Convert the garage...add a carport

Like many others, the garage formed an L with the house, so it was easy to add a carport over the driveway and convert the garage to a recreation room. Since this is a corner lot and the garage was on a side street, remodeling did not have to provide a new front entry. The emphasis was inside. The result was a room that is unusually versatile: It is a place for music and parties, for study or office work, for sewing and related activities.

To gain a full-depth storage wall without sacrificing any floor space, the architect's plans called for the cabinets to cantilever out beyond the foundation line. This device created generous space for storage, for a stereo system, and for heating ducts.

Architect: Raymond Lloyd.

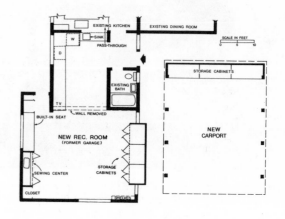

New room *opens to kitchen beyond pass-through. Counter houses sink, laundry, storage cabinets, television. Dropped ceiling sections contain heating, lighting. Bookshelves are mounted on adjustable tracks.*

Cabinets *protrude beyond wall to gain their storage depth as shown in close-up at left. Double carport at right now shelters cars displaced from former garage. Driveway kept as paving for carport.*

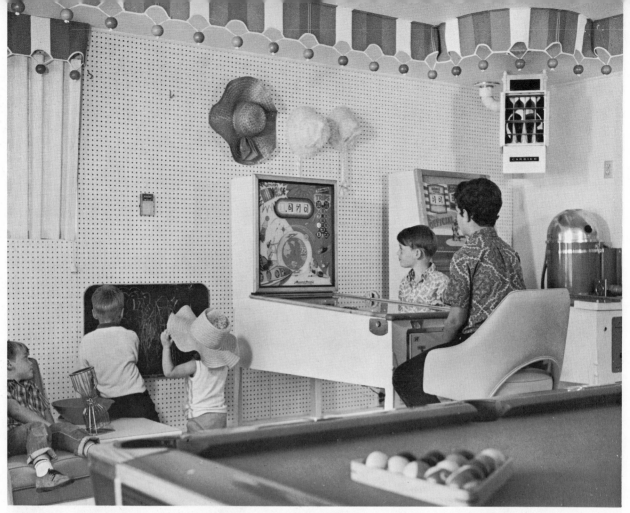

Mounting score *on pinball machine captures attention of older boys as little tots amuse themselves at the chalkboard. Space heater is shown at upper right with central vacuum system for entire house below.*

Fun for children...and adults

Equipped with two pinball machines, a mechanical bowling alley, and a pool table (all purchased as used equipment from a vending machine company), this former two-car garage offers an amusement-center setting. Though the room was originally designed for their seven children, the owners long ago found it a delightful spot for adult entertaining as well.

The original overhead door and automatic device for opening and closing it were left operational for increased ventilation when needed. A hot-air heater was installed for extra warmth during the winter. Entrance to the house is on the wall opposite the large door.

Lending splashes of color to an otherwise all-white interior (for maximum light) are a tasseled canopy of orange, red, and white; orange chair-stools; and an orange and white vinyl fabric-covered couch.

One wall is covered with perforated hardboard to provide space for hanging a small chalk board and large party hats. The remaining two walls are lined with full-length storage cabinets and drawers. A dart board is mounted on the inside of the overhead door. Vinyl tile in a brick-like pattern covers the concrete floor.

Design: Paul Scranton.

Electric bowling machine *is nine feet long; sits in front of garage door (opened for this photo).*

View *from driveway shows how recreation room forms L with house; separate entrance to house behind pool table.*

Pool table *is enjoyed even by the younger children. Note door opening device above, dart board mounted on door.*

Deep drawers *hold toys, party costumes, and sporting equipment; are low enough for access by preschoolers.*

Storage cabinets *line entire length of one wall; hold games, entertainment equipment. Note convenient shelf.*

Walking *out to garden from the house and patio, this is the first view of the teahouse. Shoji frames hold insect screening — allows ventilation yet keeps out flies and night-time insects.*

It's a garden party room

For teenage entertaining, the owners built this party stage-setting in their garden. In addition to its usefulness as headquarters for entertaining, the structure is a prominent and attractive feature of the garden landscape as you look out across the lawn from the house and patio.

The teahouse was built with money the owners saved and banked in their unique "garden fund"; each month they set aside a fixed amount for garden improvements. When they got ready to spend a sum that had been accumulating for a swimming pool, the owners realized they really didn't need one, and much preferred to have a structure for recreational activities.

During the day, the teahouse is often used as a private retreat for several quiet hours of uninterrupted reading or study. In the evening, children and adults alike make full use of it for all kinds of parties, dances and other forms of recreation. Strings of Japanese lanterns and other party props are kept on hand in the teahouse.

Landscape Architect: W. Bennett Covert.

Stand-up bar *for buffet service is at one end of room.*

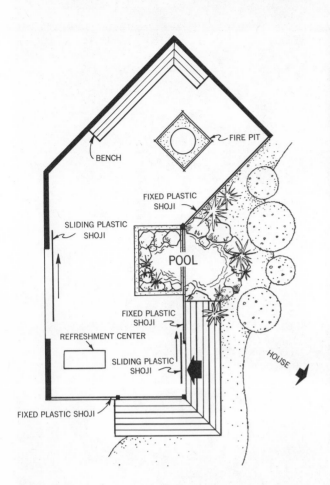

Charcoal brazier *(with legs removed) rests on bed of pebbles in masonry firepit lined with sheet copper.*

Pool water, *on recirculating system, springs from surrounding rocks; flows to waterfall, pool outside.*

Sliding glass doors *open cabaña to deck and pool beyond (note reflection in glass at left). Wicker baskets in front of couch are filled with paper flowers, covered with thick glass; act as colorful coffee tables.*

For a variety of activities...a cabaña

This five-sided outdoor room is referred to as "the cabaña" by the owners, simply because it is situated next to the swimming pool. Completely separate from the main house, it is used for a variety of activities—from teen-age parties to a quiet retreat. On three walls there are sliding glass doors that open to a deck; the swimming pool is on a lower level.

Ceiling-to-floor bookshelves along another wall provide ample space for books and games. Two bookcases are hinged to swing out for access to additional storage, a dressing room, photographic darkroom, and bath.

Along the fifth wall is a wide counter with bookshelves above and cabinets below, which accommodates arts and craft projects. At one end of the counter is a sink and built-in refrigerator. At the other end is a desk. The latter corner of the room serves as a study-home office.

An outstanding feature of the room is its free-standing, triangular fireplace, which somewhat repeats the shape of the room.

Architect: J. Martin Rosse.

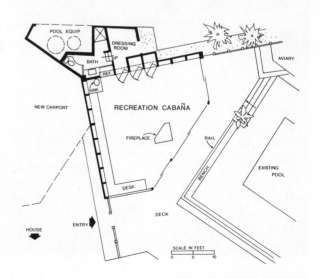

Floor area *around fireplace is convenient for children's games, and large enough for group gatherings.*

Opposite corner *contains large desk and comfortable chair. Area is used as study or quiet retreat.*

Bookcases open *to storage units, this one to deep shelves, one at left to dressing room, bath, dark room.*

Sink, built-in refrigerator *are handy for serving snacks. Gas heater (lower left) warms entire room.*

Entering *through double doors (left center), you walk through court to house entry (out of picture to right). In foreground is car shelter; it has roof, overhead door, but is open at sides; house forms rear wall.*

New carport is also a party court

This house acquired a private, walled-in court when its garage was converted to a recreation room. A new wall encloses a paved and planted area; it is used most of the time as an entry garden and a car storage area, but it is also a pleasant patio area. The owners just clean the concrete where the car has stood, then move in furniture and recreation equipment as needed.

This large court, partly roofed, combines with the new recreation room to make space for entertaining large or small groups. A storage wall at one end of the recreation room is large enough to store games, records, folding chairs, and other miscellaneous items. Sliding glass doors at the opposite end fill former garage door opening.

Architects: Matlin & Dvoretzky.

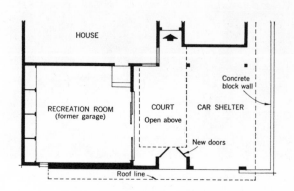

Former garage *became recreation room. Sliding glass doors replace garage door opening; open to party court.*

Before remodeling. *House was typical of many others, with an attached garage forming an L in the front.*

Garage or carport? *Door has an automatic electronic opener; inside carport the car is not visible from street.*

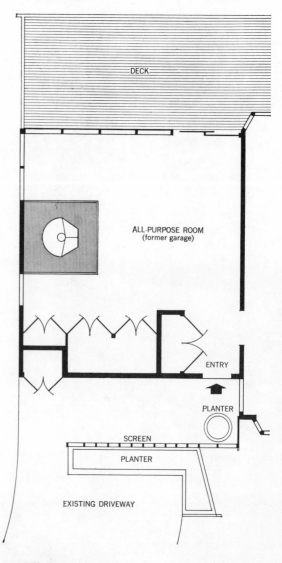

This end *of recreation room has storage wall for hi-fi components. Floor is quarry and wood-particle tile.*

Remodeling project *enlarged garage entry to kitchen, added outside entry, glass wall, deck, fireplace, storage.*

For three teen-age boys

When the three teen-age sons of the owners bring friends home, they are sent to the garage. But that's no hardship, for the garage has been remodeled into a recreation room with a separate entry, built-in hi-fi, fireplace, outdoor deck, generous storage space—and direct access to the kitchen.

A new deck extends the entire length of the new room and the existing living room; it also provides an ideal place for setting up the barbecue. When the family desires an informal eating place, table and chairs can quickly be set up at one end of the recreation room.

On the street side of the new room, a slat fence conceals the new entry and outdoor storage that remodeling provided (for garden equipment and garbage cans). The existing driveway was long enough so that the formerly-garaged cars can be parked in front of the fence screen and still provide easy access to new entry.

Architects: Mithun & Associates.

Room doubles *as informal dining room. New deck extends the entire length of the room and existing living room. Playroom has own entry, direct access to the kitchen, and a generous amount of storage space.*

Screen *on street side conceals new entry and the outdoor storage that remodeling provided (for garden equipment and garbage cans).*

Tile entry *catches most of tracked-in mud; has handy clothes closet.*

Sitting area *is two steps lower than rest of the room; half circles the large fireplace. View is beyond.*

A sitting area for entertaining

The desire to have a place where five growing children could pursue their varied activities and where guests could be entertained resulted in this striking, two-story addition. The contrast in levels between the sunken fireplace-sitting area and the balcony-mezzanine gives a feeling of two separate rooms.

Remodeling consisted of partitioning a former breakfast area into a utility room and a barbecue area that opens onto the game room. Curving from the brick, gas-fired barbecue is a wide dining counter that fronts its own service area and a pass-through to the kitchen.

Directly beneath the balcony is the generous-sized game room, with pool table, cue storage, television corner, and cabinets for miscellaneous equipment. Wicker stools and cushions are pulled up for television watching or for extra, informal seating. The character of the sitting area is enhanced by the high beamed ceiling and the massive hood of the free-standing fireplace.

The balcony leads off two bedrooms with bath between and serves as an additional game room, study area, or music center. With pull-out sofas at either end, it also does double duty as an extra bedroom.

Architects: Bakke-Cann-Page Associates.

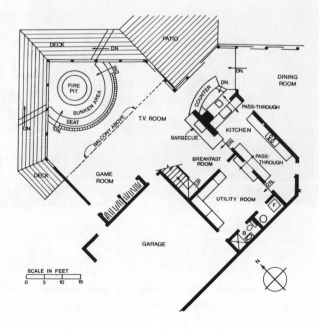

Gas barbecue *is adjacent to both recreation room and eating counter. Note balcony railing at top of photo.*

Opposite corner *has pool table, storage closets, door leading to outside. Post beam supports balcony above.*

Window wall *visually links recreation room with garden making the large room seem even bigger.*

New room *shares garden view; little furniture to move for dancing. Lights and speakers are in ceiling.*

Indoor-outdoor party room

When a family outgrows its house and the need for a large play yard, they usually move or remodel. The owners of this house decided on the latter mainly because they liked their neighborhood. Needing indoor and outdoor space for entertaining (they particularly enjoy dancing), they added a new party room and hallway-office between the house and garage. They also raised the ground level a few feet and built a terrace at floor level. Two decks were used to bridge planting beds and to link the party room and living room to this large outdoor recreation area. The decks also created a foot traffic-way. Now, besides ample space, the owners have a pleasant private garden in view of living and party room glass walls.

Design: Landscape Architect William G. Teufel.

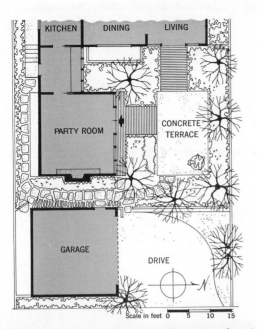

Floor and plot plan *of addition and rear garden. Note foot path leading around to the service entrance.*

Before remodeling. *House had only one access to back yard (down 3 feet via kitchen steps, shown at left).*

Decks *bridge planting to link dance room (right), raised concrete terrace, and new living room glass door (foreground), creating a large outdoor space for entertaining and foot trafficway.*

With all doors closed, *wall has handsome paneled appearance — a background for game table at one end of the recreation room. Openings in hardwood panels provide good ventilation for stereo and TV center.*

A storage wall to prevent clutter

For efficiency most architects and home planners like to locate a storage wall near party and recreation areas. They then design it in sections to take care of specific areas of interest: a sewing machine, entertainment center, a study area, etc.

Finally, by placing the whole arrangement behind large doors, as in the example shown on this page, they can avoid a cluttered look and keep things relatively dust-free.

The storage wall in this recreation room is located near the game table. It contains three sections for storing games and music, folding chairs, television tables, and other miscellaneous items. When the owners entertain, they can close the doors so the storage area looks like a paneled wall.

Architect: Wayne F. Owens.

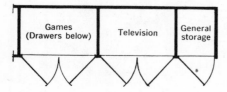

Storage wall *is an adjunct to long and narrow room. It is 10½ feet long and has three compartments.*

Behind sculptured *hardwood panels, places for games and entertainment equipment; speakers for stereo above.*

Large windows *provide good lighting even on dark days; floor area is large enough for varied activities.*

A basement recreation room

Often confining winter weather poses no problem for a family with six active children. They spend many pleasant hours in this light and airy basement recreation room.

Equipped with a ping-pong table, a built-in work counter, and a monkey bar, the place is large enough to accommodate several activities at the same time. The room is kept comfortable by radiant heat, and the polished concrete floor is ideally suited for roller skating. The walls are decorated with large travel posters; in one corner a brick fireplace, floor cushions, and an area rug add a cozy touch.

Architects: Trogdon-Smith.

Opposite end *has work counter, shelves for toy and game storage. Note upright storage cabinet at left and convenient phone extension.*

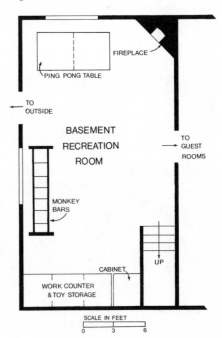

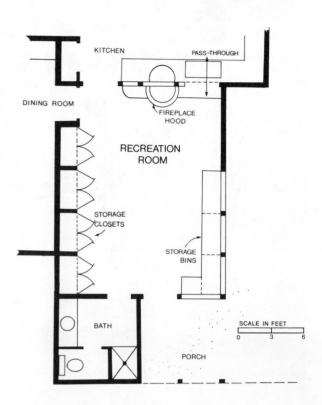

Swings *are enjoyed by younger children as well as older. Note list of rules, regulations posted on bulletin board.*

A place for high-flying activities

To the delight of the owners' five children, this two-story recreation room has room for high-flying activities as well as ground-level fun.

Both swings are secured to a ceiling beam by heavy-duty screw eyes. During the acrobatic periods, the floor is cushioned with gym mats, and an adult stands by watchfully.

Large windows in one corner of the room plus four skylights provide ample daylight even on rainy days. A generous-sized window seat runs along the entire width of the windows, the space underneath being used for storage. On the opposite wall there is a storage closet for each child, an inducement to keeping things picked up. A third wall contains a fireplace and has a pass-through to the kitchen.

Architect: Richard Sundeleaf.

Storage bins *glide on casters under the window seat. Set-back at the bottom of each bin is for toe space.*

Separate closet *for each child for toys, games. Double doors cause least congestion when open.*

FAMILY ROOMS

...for informal daily living

(See coverage of this room on page 34)

Office-studio balcony *connects with original second-story hallway. Access also by spiral stairway.*

This family room is two stories high

Ten years ago when this house was designed, the owners had future expansion clearly in mind—but at that time they weren't sure what extra space their growing family would need. As the children grew older, however, it was decided that the family's most pressing need was more room for informal entertaining, craft projects, or generally for relaxing.

What evolved is this two-story family room (which includes a balcony studio-office and a tall fireplace) built between the original house and existing carport. Outside, a deck and stairway were rebuilt and enlarged to extend along the side of the carport to the drive and provide a sheltered walkway during bad weather.

Architect: Bruce Walker.

Two-story ceiling *gives new family room the feeling of great openness. Stained cedar walls match outside siding.*

New addition *fits between the original carport at far right and existing house (see floor plans below).*

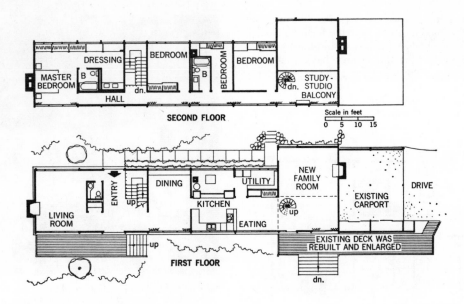

SECOND FLOOR

MASTER BEDROOM

DRESSING

B

HALL

dn.

BEDROOM

B

BEDROOM

BEDROOM

STUDY-STUDIO BALCONY

dn.

Scale in feet
0 5 10 15

FIRST FLOOR

LIVING ROOM

ENTRY

up

DINING

KITCHEN

EATING

UTILITY

up

NEW FAMILY ROOM

EXISTING CARPORT

DRIVE

EXISTING DECK WAS REBUILT AND ENLARGED

up

dn.

Ten-foot-high ceiling *adds vertical space to room. To keep bank of cabinets from looking too prominent, the architect used Douglas fir on lower doors, glass on middle ones, caning for top doors.*

Family room doubles for dining

In this house you dine at one end of the family room. But the area is so designed that you have the feeling of being in a separate room. Unlike the rest of the family room, which is mostly glass, the dining area has an intimate feeling, with wood walls broken on one side by an interesting bay window, and on the other by built-in cabinets and a marble-topped serving counter.

Architect: Clement Chen, Jr.

Sliding door *can be pulled across to close off kitchen from dining area, increasing the sense of intimacy.*

One end *of family room has display shelf wall. Picture in center conceals projection window. Note light switches on the wall at either side. The projection room is through door at left.*

Easy conversion to a home theater

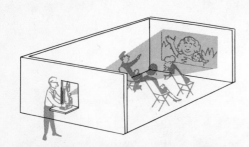

This family room beside a pool patio quickly converts to a home movie theater. At one end a large screen pulls down, darkening the end window (other openings have shutters). At the other end an adjacent projection room and storage area holds the projector in readiness, with films and extra chairs close at hand. The projection room is the size of a small closet, with a glass window to diminish projector noise.

Design: Fred Blair Green.

Opposite end *of room has alcove-like storage structure built out from wall; it contains hi-fi equipment, other gear. Note cove lighting.*

Eight-foot-wide screen *pulls down from concealment in overhead housing.*

Family room *provides floor space for play, ample work surfaces. Small table, chairs in front of counter; sewing table with storage cabinet above is at right. A light cove is at the top of the wall-hung shelves.*

A family room-kitchen combination

A similar room arrangement in their former house proved to be so satisfactory to the owners that they asked the designer to repeat the family room-kitchen design for their new house. They liked an open plan that would permit keeping an eye on three small children while working in the kitchen.

The result was this spacious (16 by 28 feet) combination family room and kitchen with special built-in furniture. All the work surfaces, including those of the family room counter, the separate table, and the counters in the kitchen, are laminated plastic in soft beige or simulated cherrywood. The walls and cabinets are cherry wood or cherry wood veneer with a natural finish.

A custom furniture maker designed the special sewing table, finished in the same materials as the room. Placed beside the eating counter-cutting table and near a built-in ironing board, it completes an efficient work center.

Design: Dallas E. Zeiger.

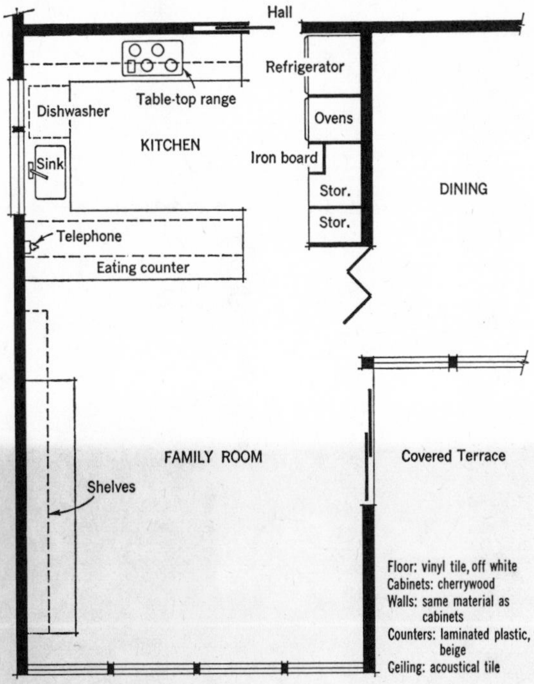
Hall
Refrigerator
Table-top range
Dishwasher
Ovens
KITCHEN
Iron board
Sink
Stor.
Stor.
DINING
Telephone
Eating counter
FAMILY ROOM
Covered Terrace
Shelves
Floor: vinyl tile, off white
Cabinets: cherrywood
Walls: same material as cabinets
Counters: laminated plastic, beige
Ceiling: acoustical tile

In plan *note sliding glass door between family room and covered terrace, to provide access to play area.*

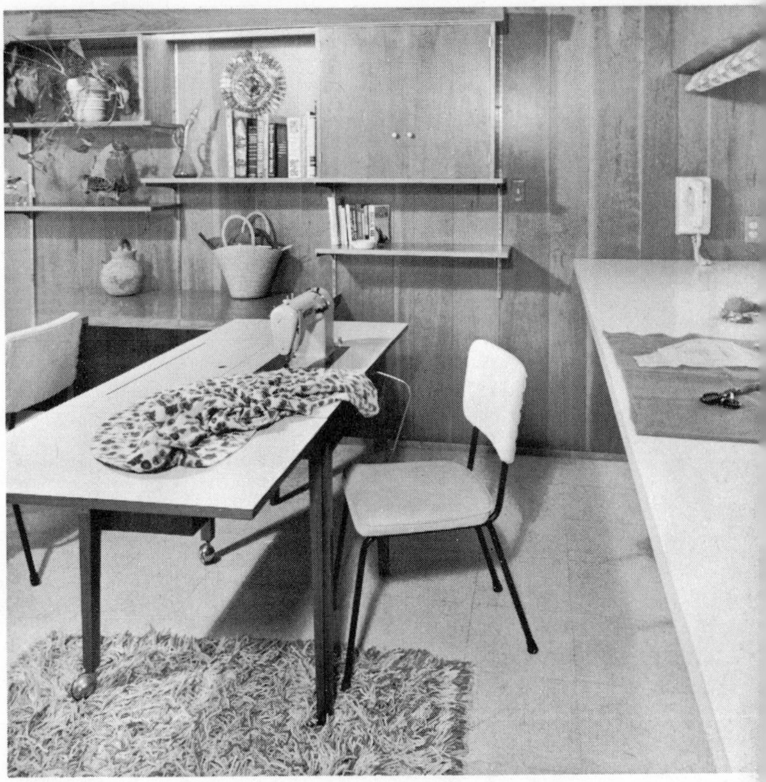

Oversized sewing table *rolls out from wall, sets up quickly. Eating counter then becomes a cutting table.*

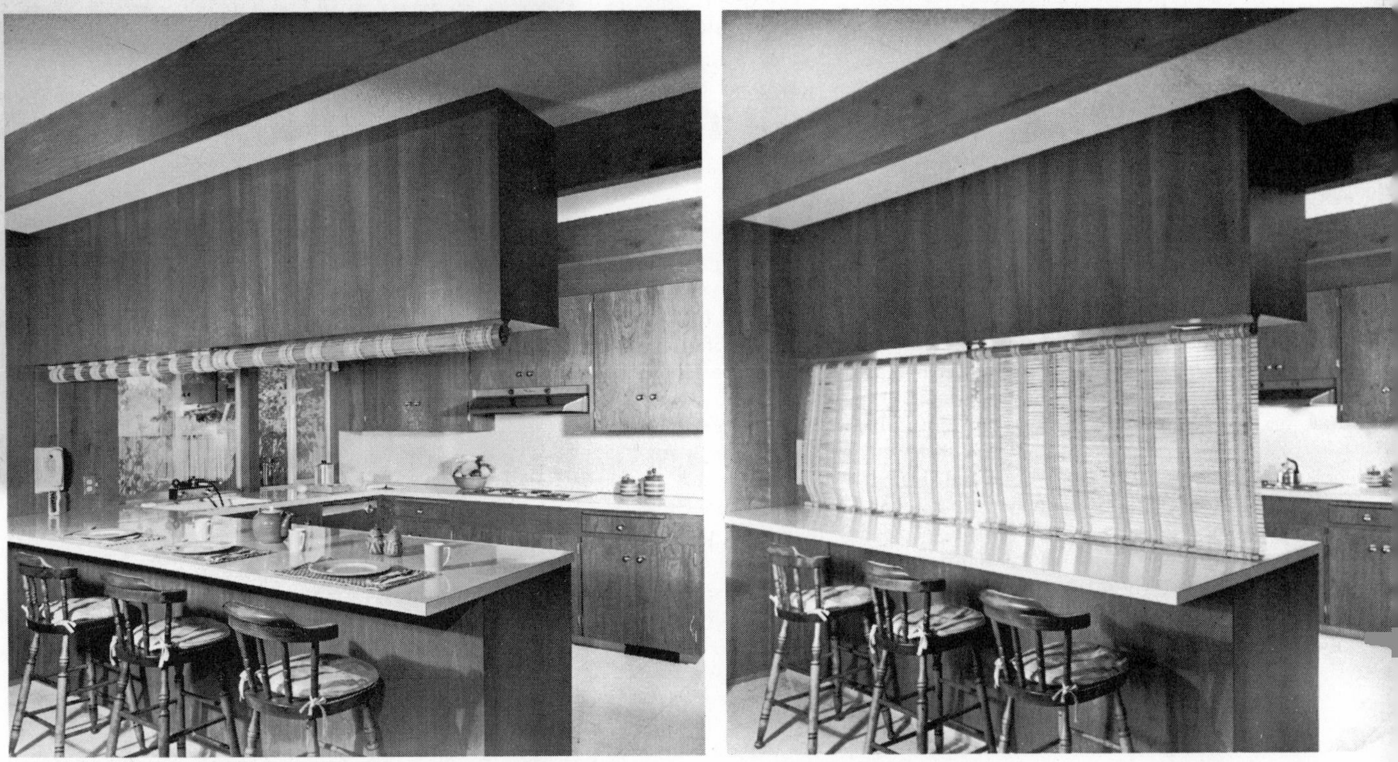

Eating counter *separates the kitchen from family room; sink and countertop range are within easy reach. Blinds of yarn and bamboo-like fiberglass strips may be lowered to conceal kitchen area from view.*

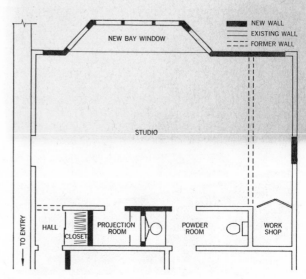

Dropped ceiling *over counter contains screen roller; hinged cover swings into place when it is retracted. Double mirrors in washroom (photo at right) swing open to light, ventilate projection room.*

It's called the family "studio"

The owners call this big family room their "studio". (For another view, see page 27.) It occupies the former garage space at one end of a long, narrow house, and thus keeps a good many working and cluttering activities in one location. Even so, it is relatively free of clutter, for the owners were able to use former storage space the length of the garage to house workshop, powder room, projection and film storage, and closet. It also seems larger than most remodeled garages, because it expanded into a former garden shed at one end.

Having an extensive slide collection, the owners drew up plans to include built-in projection facilities. A closet only 3½ by 5 feet contains the projection room. Simple shelves hold projectors and slides. A small opening in the wall places the lens about 16 feet from the screen. Even though the screen does not pull down below the counter, enough of it is exposed so slides projected are a good size when viewed from the sofa 10 feet away. The lens is exactly opposite the vertical midpoint of the screen, high enough so the light beam passes well over people seated on the sofa.

Design: Jeffrey Hayden.

Floor plan *shows how projector room, workshop, powder room, and closet line the entire length of one wall.*

Newly opened-up room *reaches back toward entry hall, living room beyond; note pass-through to kitchen.*

Three rooms became one

After the children grow up, a family often has bedrooms it no longer needs, using valuable floor space that could better serve some other use. In this house, two adjoining unused bedrooms and a hall were simply eliminated, so the space could be converted to a family-dining room complex which now makes the back garden readily accessible through doors in the new glass wall pictured below.

Architect: Jerry Gropp.

Plans show *how remodeling doubles the main living area. Another bedroom is on a lower level.*

New deck *viewed through a large glass wall helps to increase the apparent size of the family room.*

Cooking island *separates family area from kitchen; also provides work and serving space near table.*

Two walls less...one big room

In this old California-Monterey style house two walls were removed to gain a badly needed family room-kitchen area. The owners asked the designer to improve the lighting and incorporate new equipment and materials, yet keep the new room in the same tradition as the rest of the house.

The working area of the new kitchen is clearly defined, yet is a part of the family room for supervision of the children. An eating table acts as the only separation between the cooking area and the family area. A 3 by 8½-foot island with two sinks provides work and serving space near the table.

The dark oak cabinets and beams, the handcrafted tile counters, and the gray-green heavy-gauge linoleum floor retain the old California feeling.

Design: Janean.

Family area *has picture gallery along one wall; door to right leads to laundry, bath, and outside.*

Original windows *were enlarged, new ones were added, and new door to the dining room was opened beyond the right (non-cooking) side of the island. Storage to right of ovens is for dining room linens.*

Exposed beams *give family room a solid look, are good for hanging things. Note the skylight above.*

New family room and matching patio

This house was remodeled and also acquired an addition of a family room, but note how the addition retains the character of the existing structure.

Remodeling of the house involved rearranging and updating an obsolete kitchen. The addition is mainly a family room, with easy access to the outside, needed to provide more living and entertaining space for a family with four active children.

The small lavatory off the back entry (see *Before* floor plan) is gone; in its place is one entrance to the family room and a pass-through from the kitchen to the hall. This pass-through also contains a small sink and under-counter icemaker. As shown in the photograph on the opposite page, the remodeled kitchen opens to the family room, but a feeling of partial separation is achieved by a counter peninsula with cooktop and storage on both sides, and by ceiling-mounted cabinets.

Architect: Adolph S. Rosekrans.

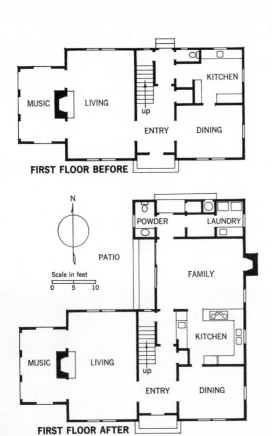

FIRST FLOOR BEFORE

MUSIC LIVING KITCHEN

ENTRY DINING

up

N

PATIO

Scale in feet
0   5   10

POWDER LAUNDRY

FAMILY

KITCHEN

MUSIC LIVING

ENTRY DINING

up

FIRST FLOOR AFTER

Peninsula counter top *is wood so it can be used for chopping, cutting; small area rugs cushion floor.*

New addition, *at left, opens directly to brick patio through sliding glass door. Partly open square window is in the new half bath. Outside appearance of new room retains character of existing house.*

The addition doubled their floor space

By using space that had been carport and driveway, the owners of this house gained a large family room plus a master bedroom and bath, and a new utility room. A new carport at the front of the house provides parking places for two cars. The new family room has a built-in home office behind double doors, storage space under the eating counter, window walls on two sides, and sliding doors opening to the terrace. A minimum amount of furniture keeps floor space free for children's play.

Architects: Bystrom and Greco.

Well lighted *family room has large eating counter.*

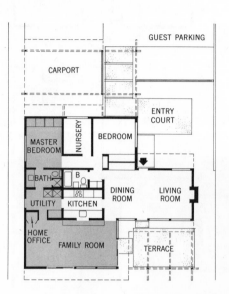

They kept the Mediterranean look

This roomy, well-built Mediterranean-style house needed extra space to suit the owners to family living today. Not all older houses come through this type of remodeling as gracefully as the one shown here. Though updated inside and out, it still retains much of its characteristic Spanish-American flavor.

Architects: Benton & Park.

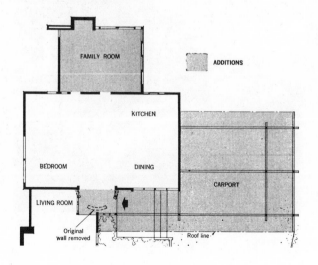

At the rear, *family room opens onto spacious patio.*

Patio became the family room

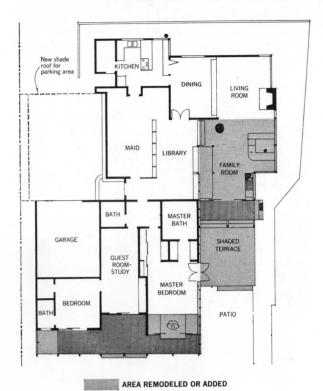

To meet the need for more floor space, the architect designed a family room at the same level as the existing living room, 18 inches lower than the floor in the rest of the house. His design removed the wall between the living and dining rooms to open the two rooms, and opened the new family room to the library (former music room).

Architect: Carl Day.

AREA REMODELED OR ADDED

Former patio area *became family room; has barbecue.*

Family-dining area big enough for parties

A new design for the wing of their house that reached back into the garden gave the owners new livability suited to their needs while preserving the character of the fine old house and garden. They now have a family-dining area big enough for parties, teen-age gatherings of their two older daughters, and activities of their pre-school daughter; a big kitchen; a bedroom and bath. A glass wall now brings the garden in and they can move easily out onto a floor-level deck which is L-shaped.

Architect: H. Douglas Byles.

New family room *also serves for parties, dancing.*

The built-in units free floor space

By converting half the space of their two-car garage, the owners gained a long family room. By designing and installing built-in units they provided work space for themselves and furniture-free play space for their small daughter. Part of the original wall between kitchen and garage was removed and the line of kitchen cabinets continued into the new room. A 6-foot-long section of floor-to-ceiling cabinets provides storage space for cleaning equipment. In the desk-bookcase unit on the opposite wall the sewing machine is stored behind the fold-down desk top. Beneath the desk on the left are pull-out file drawers.

Design: Norman V. Manoogian.

Bookcase wall *has desk area, with storage above, below.*

Cabinet *has slot cut in shelf to hold ironing board.*

Additional room for a growing family

Not wanting to move because they liked their location, but needing additional room, prompted the owners to enlist the help of an architect to work out the solution shown on this page. Floor space devoted to kitchen use stayed the same, but the new family room addition provided ample space for the varied interests and activities of a growing family (see floor plan).

Architect: Robert Theriault.

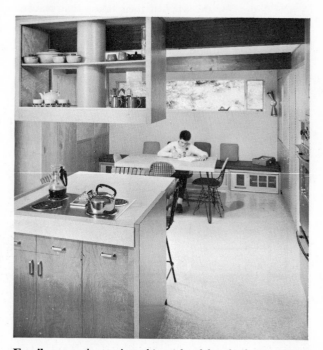

Family room *beyond cooking island has built-in storage.*

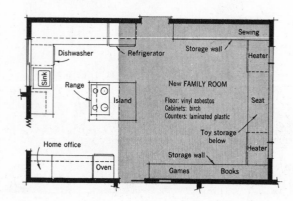

Shaded area *is new family-room extension of kitchen.*

SEWING CENTERS

...for the serious or part~time seamstress

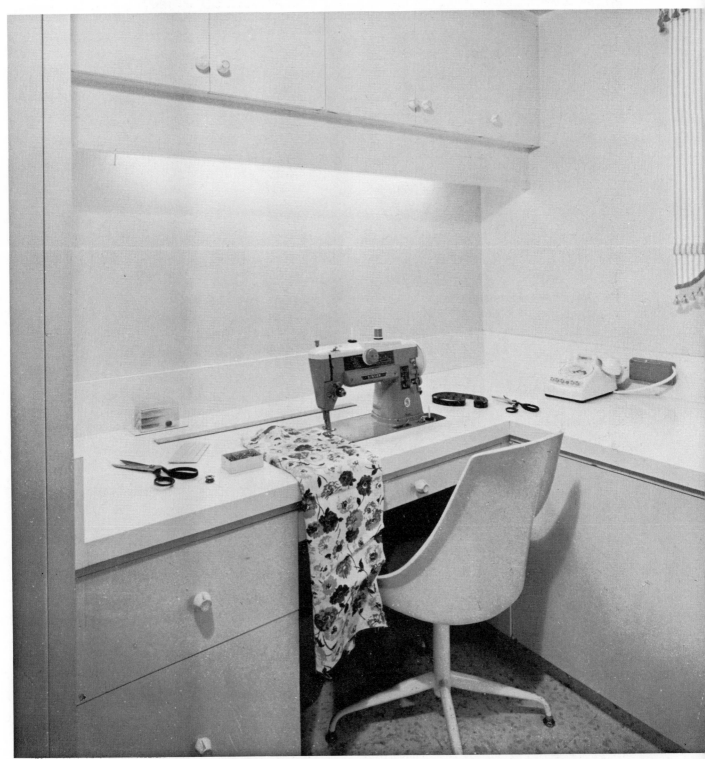

(See coverage of this center on page 48)

Top *of wall-hung cabinet also serves as a buffet counter along one wall of the dining area.*

It matches the other furniture

The seamstress can leave work in progress at any time on the inner counter of this 9-foot-long cabinet, then lower the top to hide the clutter. The architect designed it in walnut plywood to match other cabinets in a combination family room-kitchen-dining area, and faced the top and inside counters with laminated plastic. The sewing machine is a portable one that plugs into a wall outlet just below the cabinet. Storage space below the work top is generous with adjustable shelves and pull-out trays.

Architect: Frank Shell.

Patterns *can be tacked to cork. Counter is generous: storage below includes pull-out trays, adjustable shelves.*

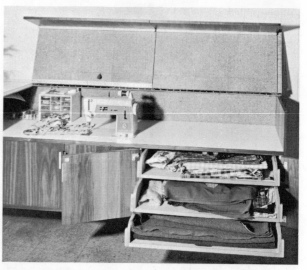

Cabinet top *lifts in three cork-lined sections; when closed, it clears machine with the thread holder removed.*

Sewing table *top pulls out from the wall so fabric will drop over the edge.*

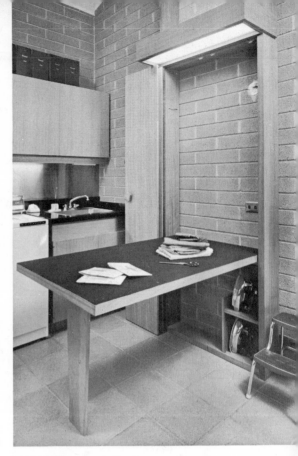

Cutting table *unfolds from cupboard.*

A combination sewing-laundry room

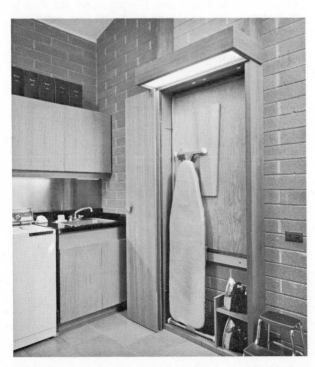

Ironing board *stores in cupboard along with folded-up cutting table. Laundry center includes sink.*

In this combination room, everything for both sewing and laundry is concentrated in one place. Several of the ideas shown here could be duplicated in a smaller space. The base of the sewing table, with a knee-hole, is permanently built-in. Its plywood top, covered with plastic laminate, rests on two stationary, box-like supports, and slides forward so material can drop behind the machine.

Because of leisure time for sewing projects at the owner's summer cabin, the cut-out section in the counter top is designed so the machine can be disconnected, lifted out, and taken along.

The storage cupboard for the cutting table and ironing board is 7 feet high. Its sides are floor-to-ceiling 2 by 8's. The table, 32 inches wide and 54 inches long, stores flat against the wall, held by spring steel fasteners. It folds down on a piano hinge. The cutting table is covered in felt so fabrics won't slip while cutting. The ironing board is held in place by a short coiled spring attached with screws to the underside of the table. Above the cupboard a translucent plastic panel diffuses light from several standard light bulbs. A bi-folding door on piano hinges conceals the storage.

The laundry center to the left of the storage cupboard includes a sink for pre-soaking clothes and hand washing. The proximity of the washer and dryer to the storage cupboard enables the cutting table to be used as a sorting-folding area when needed.

Architect: William A. Patrick.

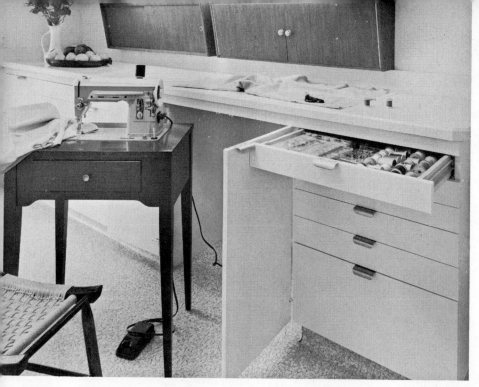

Sewing counter: *Console machine fits under counter which now serves as cutting table. Drawers to the right hold sewing supplies.*

Across from counter, *closet stores this dress form and other supplies.*

A sewing-wrapping counter

A sewing-wrapping counter is part of this utility room with washer and dryer, laundry tray or flower sink, and plenty of storage space. The counter is big enough to lay out a full dress length of fabric and has space below to store the sewing machine (which folds down into its own cabinet). Drawers to the right hold sewing accessories and the sewing chair stores underneath the machine.

In space ordinarily not used between the counter top and the upper cabinets, the owner hung two long, narrow cabinets with slanting fronts (deeper at the top than at the bottom). These cabinets hold wrapping paper and ribbons and when needed the counter directly below becomes the wrapping desk.

Design: Louis Mazzetti.

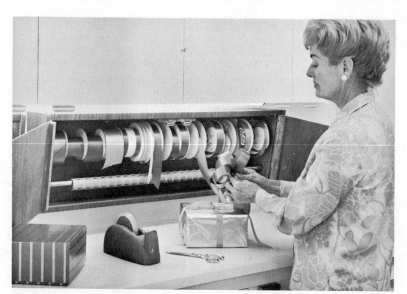

Wrapping counter: *Ribbon, paper hung on dowels are easy to use in shallow cupboard with wide doors. Fluorescent lights under top cabinets.*

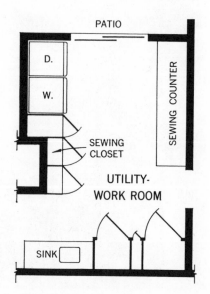

Sewing-wrapping counter *is part of utility room with washer, dryer.*

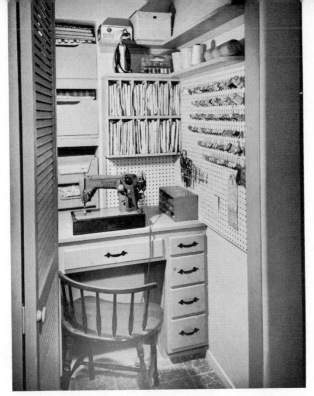

Sewing alcove *in unused closet has built-in table with overhead skylight. Vertical dividers store patterns.*

Storage unit *pulls out of cabinet, machine lifts into place in this sewing alcove. Archs.: Matlin & Dvoretzky.*

They were designed to save space

All those who sew would agree—sewing equipment should be stored where you use it. Often such an arrangement can be worked out in very little space. For example, the sewing center at right above fits into a small alcove. The storage unit for the machine pulls out like a drawer, the top section folds down to provide extra counter space, and the machine head lifts up into sewing position. In the sewing closet at left above, perforated hardboard is used for hanging spools of thread, the divided section for patterns, the bins for materials. If the cabinet design of a console machine no longer fits your decor, you may be able to make it look like a piece of built-in equipment—like the console shown at right below. The sewing center at left below is simply concealed in a closet.

Closet holds *console, chair; adjustable shelves above; lower shelf is tilted. Archs.: Liebhardt and Weston.*

Machine stands *between storage drawers; cutting table is at right. Archs.: Lillis & Smith.*

1. **Kitchen counter** *has fold-down sewing machine, cupboards at right for supplies, additional counter space at left. With the machine folded into space below, the counter becomes a place for quick lunches, menu planning, and home office work. Arch.: Germano Milono; Interior Design: Virginia Lewis.*

Sewing centers that lead a double life

Here are four quite different examples of efficient sewing center planning. In each case the sewing machine can be ready for use in a matter of seconds, and all the paraphernalia that accompanies a sewing project is stored close by. When it's not being used for sewing, each example serves some other purpose.

In the kitchen arrangement (1), the seamstress can use the kitchen counter—or the cook can use the sewing counter. The sewing alcove (2) is a remodeled breakfast room. The wall-hung, fold-down sewing table (3) done in teak and mahogany, is especially versatile, and could be adapted to many locations. The combination laundry-sewing center (4) is practical for a family with small children. It has the added advantage of serving as a snack bar at one end of an open-air play area that takes advantage of a mild climate.

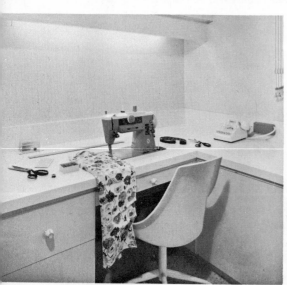
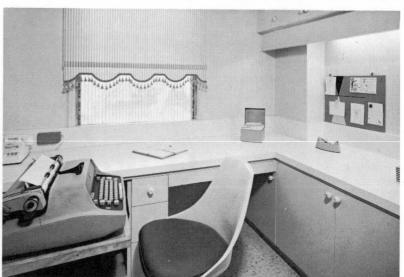

2. **Built-in sewing machine** *is always in place on left side of U-shaped counter in alcove off kitchen. Fluorescent tube (behind baffle) sheds clear light on work surface. For office use, chair rolls back, typewriter pulls out on pop-up platform. Note telephone and bulletin board. Archs.: Matlin & Dvoretzky.*

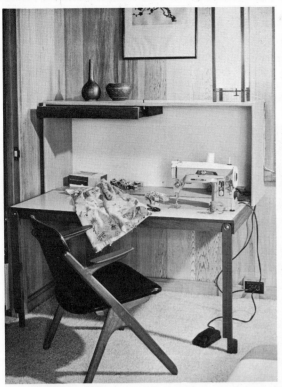
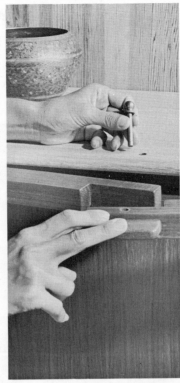

3. **Sewing machine** *is permanently mounted to fold-down table in master bedroom. Shallow drawer holds sewing accessories. Table folds up to form wall-hung cabinet: cabinet front-rear depth is same as machine height. Jog on right table leg becomes pull. Center photo shows locking device. Design: Tom Hirai.*

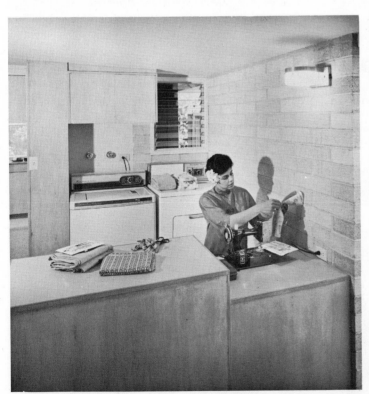

4. **Two-level cabinet** *in this open-air sewing-laundry area was designed to accommodate stand-up and sit-down sewing; includes laundry bins, drawer for sewing supplies. At family parties, children are served at counter. Adjacent to open play area, it also serves as refreshment center. Arch.: Alfred Preis.*

A fold-down table for mending

Because of the small size of the room, this sewing counter was designed to fold up out of the way when not in use. When needed the sewing machine can be set up quickly for mending clothes right from the dryer. The sewing counter often doubles as a table when there are more children for lunch than the kitchen eating counter can accommodate.

Architects: Rushmore and Woodman.

Machine *can be set up quickly for mending clothes right from dryer. Counter often doubles as eating counter.*

Counter folds *up out of the way when not in use. Down, it allows access to shallow storage shelves.*

Built into a 5-foot square

A sewing corner close to the washer, dryer, and ironer can sometimes be built into the corner of the utility room as the one shown here. It covers a little more than half of a 5-foot square. Counter space is 20 inches deep. Drawers on each side of the work space are of varying depth, divided by partitions for spools of thread and other sewing items. The sewing machine can be stored underneath the counter when not in use.

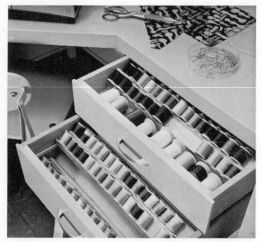

Sewing corner *built into utility room covers a little more than half of a 5-foot square. Counter space is 20 inches deep. Spool drawers have slanted, sliding trays. Top drawer has special tray for larger spools.*

HOME OFFICES
...for large and small projects

(See coverage of this office on page 58)

Modified for special needs

Many people would undoubtedly like to have a work room or home office that would operate like an old roll-top desk—by pulling down a lid, all the clutter would magically disappear. The next best thing to this idealistic dream is to have a special room set aside for office use, without robbing needed space from other rooms. And if this isn't feasible, mounting a hollow-core door on a wall bracket (or devising a table that pulls down from the wall) may provide all the elbow room and counter space that is needed for working on a hobby or project, or just keeping up with the mundane job of paying bills.

The half-dozen work areas shown on these two pages have been designed or modified to suit the particular needs of the person or persons using them. Two were designed into their owners' homes when they were built, three resulted from remodeling projects, and one occupies temporary space in a studio that will eventually be converted into a master bedroom.

Ranch home office *is where the owners keep records, take care of pear orchard business. Drawer, file space more important than open counters. Arch.: John M. Payne.*

Office-painting studio *is close by the kitchen, so users can work and chat with the cook, yet be out of the way. Stairwell separates the two. Archs.: Terry & Moore.*

Old bay window *has 9-foot counter in this husband-and-wife office. Former window at right now has shelves. Note bulletin board. Design: John B. Matthias.*

Temporary home office *for architect has ample counter space for chess, architectural homework. Space will become master bedroom. Arch.: Richard Banta.*

Research and study center *in this house has desk near wall of bookshelves (with handy ladder for the high ones). Archs.: James Widrig and David Wright.*

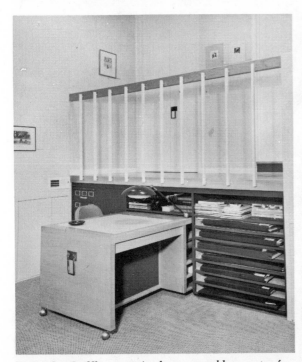

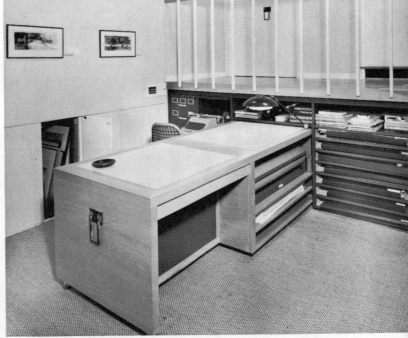

Lower-level office *contains large movable counter for sorting prints, wrapping (note roll of wrapping paper underneath). Shelves at right hold prints; typewriter, file drawers are at opposite end. When space is not needed, part of counter rolls into dead space created by the office addition. Arch.: Robert Garland, Jr.*

There's a garden in the office

A street-level office and a garden deck seem to flow together in this home of a landscape architect and his artist wife. Double doors to the deck, which faces due south, can be open much of the year, allowing them to enjoy their garden even during working hours.

Design: Gordon Drake.

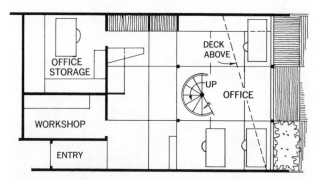

Mahogany-plywood cabinets *give ample storage. Walls are white; beams and rafters are a dull blue. Flourishing tropical plants bring garden indoors. Floor plan shows relation to upper level living area.*

Glass wall *separates office from garden deck. Floor is redwood block on concrete. Header pattern also in deck.*

Office is open *to floor above; gets full benefit of two-story glass wall. Matchstick bamboo provides shade.*

It uses every inch of space

This built-in desk uses every inch of potential drawer space—including a corner section that usually ends up as dead storage. It was designed to fit into a small alcove off the master bedroom. The office occupies a space only 4 feet by 7 feet.

Architect: Morgan Stedman.

Two-drawer unit *rolls out of space in corner (usually left as dead space); each drawer rolls forward.*

Track *for drawer unit is fastened under the desk counter. Knob on the left side is used to pull out unit.*

Knee hole *is ample with drawer unit pushed back into space in corner. Office occupies space 4 feet by 7 feet.*

This office goes into hiding

The clutter in the corner of this home office is neatly concealed when three stacking screens are pulled out. Formerly a garage, the room was transformed with the addition of 8-foot-high rosewood wall paneling, sound-absorbing ceiling tiles, and tough outdoor carpeting over the concrete floor. In case the owners wish to use it as a garage again, the garage door is intact.

Design: David R. Harkness.

Recessed track *is hung between two 2 by 6's a foot below ceiling; screens stack to right for access to office.*

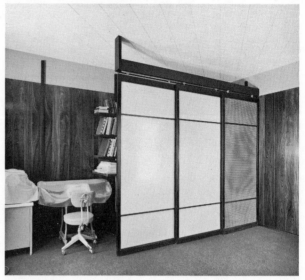

Screens *are panels of translucent fiberglass-reinforced plastic (decorative metal covers third one).*

A sitting room~bedroom~office

Office-sitting room *with fireplace can double for entertaining small groups. It is furnished with cherry and cane furniture. Blue-greens predominate. Sliding doors can close off the bedroom area. Arch.: Burr Richards.*

Efficient use of limited space

This disappearing office provides for highly efficient use of limited space. A swivel chair makes it easy to turn from the typing and filing side to the opposite desk with phone, adding machine, and upper book shelf. Lighting can be adjusted with three bullet-type lights. Double folding birch doors with sturdy brass knobs slide on a track above to hide the office from view.
Design: Ward D. Anderson.

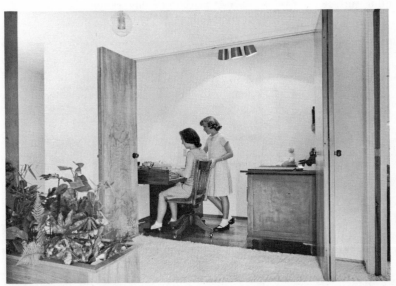 

Closet-sized *home office measures 106½ inches long, 50 inches deep. Laminated plastic shelves are work surfaces, support typewriter, left, cover desk, right. Double folding doors hide the office from view.*

Compact office in an alcove

Tucked *into hall alcove, this home office has desk built around standard file drawers, storage shelves above.*

From living room, *desk is completely hidden. Half-wall gives feeling of space. Arch.: Helen Rysdale.*

A hideaway office

Taking up just the space of a typical closet, this home office can be kept tidy or not; a pair of folding doors rapidly closes it off when not in use. Its 2½ by 6½-foot space holds a generous 30-inch-high desk, supported on one end by a two-drawer filing cabinet. The desk top is wood-grained laminated plastic, a good writing surface and one that is easy to keep clean.

A tier of cabinets with pull-down doors built on the upper right wall provides additional storage. Working light comes from a ceiling fixture. A plug-in jack makes it easy to move the telephone in or out. For seating, a comfortable leather chair has only to be swung around from its normal place in the library-television room.

Design: John F. Jennings.

Opening *off a corner of the den, this closet-sized office contains a 30-inch-high desk, file cabinet below and storage drawers above. Folding doors paneled in same material as walls conceal office from view.*

A utility area was converted

In their subdivision home, the owners did not install a washer and dryer (for just the two of them) and converted a utility room into this spacious home office. Counter is standard 36-inch height so appliances can be installed later if desired.

Design: John Garmany.

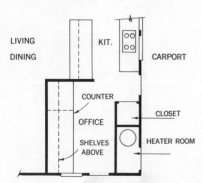

Counter *is made of hollow-core doors, covered with plastic laminate and supported by angle braces.*

Office area *has direct access to out-of-doors. Large window over counter provides plenty of light.*

A two-story studio office

Lighted *from above by a skylight, two-story office is on opposite side of house from children's play area.*

Gallery *is structural link of office with upper level of house; main entryway is to the left of stairs.*

An office retreat

A home office in a separate building provides the owner a quiet retreat for research and study. The large room has a free-standing fireplace, and is lined with bookshelves. The pool table, when covered, also doubles as a work surface when needed. (For complete coverage of this room, see page 14.)

Architect: J. Martin Rosse.

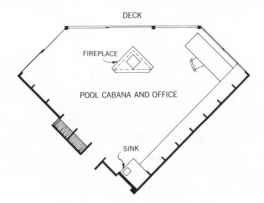

Custom-made top *on a steel desk frame extends work surface and forms L with counter and bookshelves.*

Four more office ideas

Extra wall space *in master bedroom is used for this built-in home office. Typewriter shelf swings up from storage cabinet below desk. Archs.: Benton & Park.*

Corner of family room *has a built-in home office behind double doors. Adjustable shelves above desk, drawers below, store supplies. Archs.: Bystrom and Greco.*

Guest room doubles *as home office with a 2 by 8½-foot laminated plastic counter supported by angle braces. Acoustical ceiling absorbs sound. Design: Cliff May.*

Desk alcove *is tucked out of the way in this family room. Bookshelves, storage cabinets, typewriter, and telephone all within easy reach. Arch.: H. Douglas Byles.*

STUDIOS & WORKSHOPS
...for artists and home craftsmen

(See coverage of this studio on page 65)

Part-time painter's studio *added to main house is simple and well equipped for artist's needs.*

A well-equipped painting studio

This 10 by 12-foot addition to an existing house gave the owner a well-equipped studio for her interest in painting. It includes an extra-high, 12-foot-long work counter and an 8-foot-long sink counter, both surfaced with wood-grained plastic laminate; a red vinyl tile floor; and off-white painted walls and ceiling. Fully-insulated, it's warmed by a portable heater (instead of radiant heat as in the house). A door connects it with the kitchen. It has one small light over the sink and two 8-foot-long fluorescent tubes along the main overhead beam. A perforated hardboard panel provides hanging space for pictures. Sliding glass doors let in daylight from the northwest.

Storage *below the 39-inch-high counter is open; will handle most shapes and sizes of canvas.*

Studio ties *in with house, shares the garden view. Sliding doors face the northeast for additional light.*

Studio floats *above its site on slope behind house. Wall on left is faced with cork for displaying paintings.*

High on a hill...a studio retreat

Wall-length counter *is at good height for standing, sitting. Cabinet shelves hold large sheets of paper.*

Because the best place to build this workroom-studio hideaway was on a hillside about 40 feet behind and 15 feet above the rear terrace, large machinery could not be moved in and all materials had to be carried up by hand.

The architects, therefore, designed the building with a minimum of concrete work and with no masonry or plastering. A simple space of about 18 by 22 feet, its three continuous floor beams rest on posts on concrete piers. Three similar wood roof beams support wood rafters gently tapered at the end for a light roof line. Three of the walls are of stud construction with horizontal redwood siding; a fourth wall is of glass. Inside, one wall is a display wall, one is all high cabinets (with glass above for a balance of daylighting), and one is a working wall with counter and cabinets.

The result is a spacious studio secluded from the house, where the owners can pursue their hobbies of oil painting, mosaics, sculpture, and photography. One practical aspect of their pleasant seclusion is that it is not necessary to clean up at the end of each working period.

Architects: Benton & Park.

Over-all view *of studio: Window is on north; end wall of cork has skylight equipped for nightlighting.*

Storage cabinets, *built for canvases, have shelves and vertical compartments with pull-out drawer above.*

Added: a multi-purpose studio

The location of this house and its proximity to good schools and shopping prompted the owner to remodel rather than move in order to achieve the space she needed. An active painter, she wanted a studio and, in addition, private outdoor living space and less lawn and garden to care for.

By adding the studio at the back of the house, the architect cut the rear garden area in half and gave it summertime protection from the north wind. French doors connect a new deck with the dining room, and the new studio with the garden.

The studio, equipped to handle the materials of a serious painter, also serves as a study for the owner's teen-age daughters, and as an occasional guest room and meeting place for neighborhood groups.

Architect: Nathan Wilkinson, Jr.

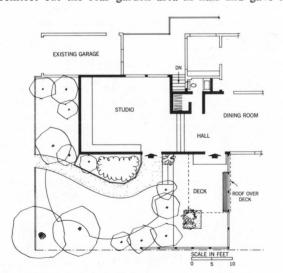

Studio reduced *lawn area; elongated walk leads to new deck and outside entrance of studio.*

Single beds recess *partly under the storage cabinets, are easily pulled out for overnight guests.*

Burlap display wall *with tube lighting recessed overhead, a couch, and lauhala mat on the floor, all lend pleasant touches to livability of studio. Note lift-top drawing table and adjustable lamp.*

Studio with 24-hour livability

For an artist who works at home, this unit offers 24-hour livability. It contains a well-lighted work area, a small bedroom, and bath. A separate entrance allows the owner to bypass activities in the main part of the house, and to work undisturbed by household traffic.

To keep surfaces uncluttered, there are many close-at-hand drawers and built-in shelves for the variety of materials an artist needs.

Architects: Dennis, Slavsky and Whitaker.

Canvases dry *without smearing in deep wall slots, left, in varying sizes. Skylight provides north light.*

Addition *above carport gives the studio a sense of isolation; has bedroom and bath-dressing room.*

Directional light *comes from glass wall; general light from fluorescent lamps. Storage island has counter top where artist works; sit-down counter is at left. Hardboard sliding doors close cabinets.*

Good storage, lighting, and work space

This studio, the domain of the sculptor-mosaicist owner, is full of ideas for planning a studio workshop. It is secluded, has ample storage, and provides good lighting close to generous work areas. The architect designed it to be structurally a part of the carport and half its size.

Architect: Perry Johanson.

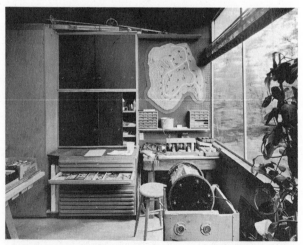

One end *of workshop has equipment for tumbling, grinding, polishing rocks. Cabinets above hold lapidary tools.*

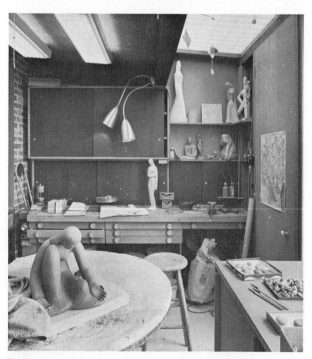

Bullet lamps *increase light for close work. Three work surfaces close together give room to spread out.*

Sliding glass doors *open to large atrium for increased light, ventilation. Loom sits in center of room.*

Spool rack *stands to left of storage closet. Warping board is attached to wall (out of picture at left).*

The extra bedroom is a weaving studio

An extra bedroom with an entrance to the outside as well as one to an inside hall serves as a weaving studio and sometime-painting-studio. Sliding glass doors open to a light and airy atrium to give a feeling of additional space. A large window on the opposite wall is shuttered to increase or decrease light as needed. Under the window is a counter with file drawers, which holds a small loom for making sample materials.

A former clothes closet stores the voluminous amount of yarns, threads, and other equipment used by the artist-owner. Not shown in the photos, but attached to a third wall is a warping board.

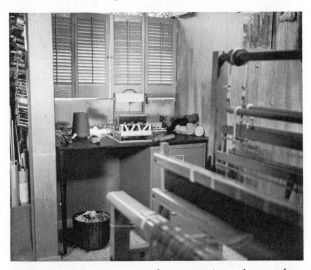

Small table loom *sits on work counter; is used to work up sample colors and designs for tapestries.*

Hanks of yarn *are hung on separate dowels which are inserted into long board and attached to wall.*

Work counter *runs along one wall, provides ample space for lapidary equipment, studying, aquarium (out of picture at right), other craft projects. Underneath, narrow drawers pull out, store papers, small objects.*

They added a family craft center

For a family interested in crafts, this large (18 x 19 feet) owner-designed room provides enough area for handling several projects at a time.

The addition uses space formerly occupied by a rear patio and flower bed. One door connects with the kitchen, the other opens onto a deck overlooking the garden. A large window floods the room with daylight. Adjustable, wall-mounted lamps and ceiling lights are used at night. Extending the full length of one wall is a formica counter with shallow drawers. Another wall has three ceiling-to-floor storage closets, one of which contains a sewing center. A fourth wall is covered with sheet cork, used as a gigantic display board for finished projects and mementoes. The floor is vinyl tile.

A sturdy table which can be extended for large projects, along with a vinyl fabric-covered couch and chair, pull-up chairs, and stereo unit, make up the furnishings for this family craft center.

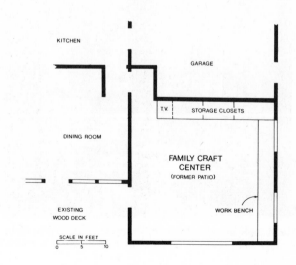

Painting corner *is well lighted by windows on each side; adjustable lamp on wall is used for nightlighting.*

Table *in center of room can be extended for working on larger projects; top is simulated-wood formica.*

Cork wall *serves as gigantic bulletin board for displaying finished craft items and hanging wet paintings to dry. Small cabinet below shelves at right stores portable television. Book shelves are above.*

Tools and supplies *are close at hand in workshop; even with cars inside there is plenty of working room.*

Long garden tools *store in cabinet at left, toxic chemicals above. Power mower fits below countertop, right.*

Garage workshop~garden shop

A garage workshop can be made pretty cheerful, rather than a cluttered, gloomy corner as this example shows.

This garage started out with bare stud walls and no ceiling. The owner paneled the walls himself with prefinished ¼-inch lauan plywood. He also added a suspended ceiling for insulation, sound control, and good lighting (this ceiling installation is described in the chapter on HOW-TO-DO-IT IDEAS).

The shop's upper cabinets and tool boards are hung on the plywood walls with screws, so they can be reshuffled as desired. The single shelf above these upper cabinets is kept available for boards currently being used, and for partially completed projects.

The two workbenches are similar to kitchen base cabinets, except they are not attached to the walls. They hold tools and supplies in drawers and on shelves. Bench tops are ¼-inch hardboard glued over ¾-inch plywood. The hardboard tops are literally saturated with a floor wax, so glue and paint won't adhere.

Garage walls alongside the cars are kept free so car doors can open—on one side there's only a folding drafting table and on the other is the shallow tool storage shown on the opposite page. The grinder shelf there is half of a sink "cutout". Note how a ¼-inch drill is stored close at hand in a hole through the shelf. Also note the two switches above the grinder. Out of a small child's reach, they turn off the power to all tool outlets in the garage. Another switch controls lighting.

The patio at the rear is a real asset. The 6-foot-high fence hides potting materials, a garden tiller, fireplace wood. A 4-inch layer of gravel keeps it dry underfoot while hosing off garden equipment.

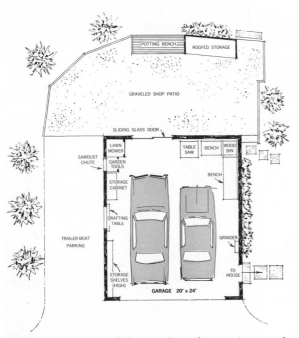

Garage *contains workshop and garden equipment, has sliding glass doors leading to own private patio.*

Shallow shelves *(9½ inches deep) on left side of garage door; canvas awning gaily covers all supplies.*

Large plywood box *rolls into shop corner, holds both usable scraps, kindling. Hinged top gives extra work counter.*

Case *for multi-use tool hangs on wall; shelf holds drill, grinder in shallow area where car door is opened.*

Stationary tools *are placed at an angle to handle large lumber. Wall at right encloses a paint-spray room, small bathroom. Cabinets and bench along this side are for tools and supplies, not woodworking.*

For the all-out woodworking hobbyist

This 19 by 36-foot shop was designed basically for woodworking. The size of the shop and its supplies permit production in quantity, so that when the owner sets up the lathe to make a large bowl, he turns several instead of one.

For Christmas gifts one year, he band-sawed 20 large salad fork and spoon sets. The owner has stored rare hardwoods in every spare inch of space.

Architect: Frank Lloyd Wright.

Opposite side *contains 33-foot long woodworking bench with fluorescent and spot lighting above.*

Handy rolls *of polyethylene, kraft, and corrugated paper (for wrapping, painting) are kept above a cabinet.*

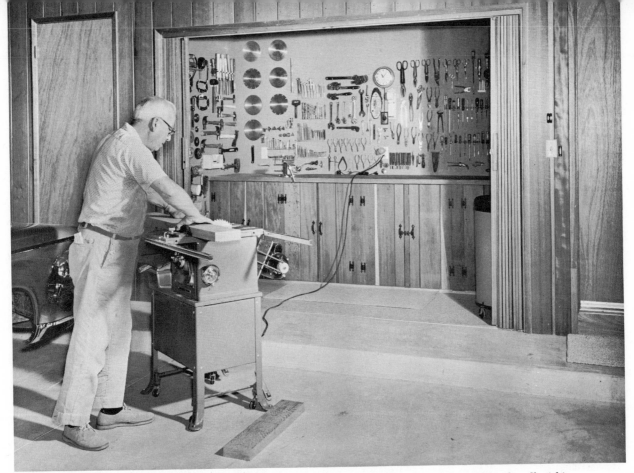

Accordion-fold doors *open up on neat workbench with small tools hung above on screws and hooks, all within easy reach. Power saw rolls out for use, otherwise stays behind the doors.*

This workshop completely disappears

In a space only 5 by 10 feet at the back of the garage, the owner has built a remarkably uncluttered and efficient workshop. Small tools, individually hung from screws and hooks, store neatly on the three inner walls. Under the workbench top, cabinet doors conceal shelves and drawers that hold power tools, hardware, nails and screws, other supplies. The floor is covered with cushioned material for comfortable standing.

Drawers *under workbench hold 82 tin containers for nails and screws.*

Closing tight *to form an uncluttered wall, the Philippine mahogany doors can be locked securely when the workshop is not in use.*

Flip-top counter for an artist

On this work counter, the owner can mix paints, stretch canvas, or build frames; then by flipping up a section of the counter, she can uncover a sink and wash brushes and palettes. Like many other artists and craftsmen, she frequently has to improvise special conveniences to meet specific work needs. The top of the counter is 36 inches high, and the sink is 32 inches, allowing enough space between the two for the water faucets.

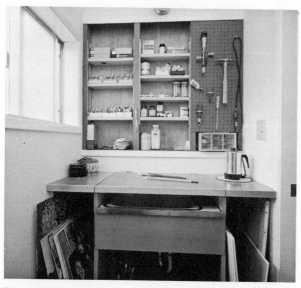

Plywood counter *makes a 45½ x 19½-inch working surface. Adjustable shelves in back for paints, supplies.*

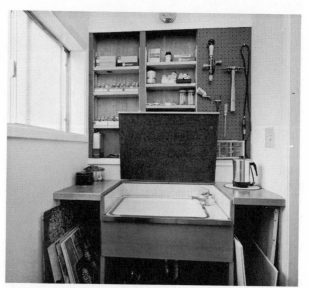

Hinged section *flips up to reveal sink for washing, cleaning brushes; note slots below for paintings, canvas.*

A workshop for father and son

This home workshop is a modest room alongside the owner's garage. It's full of tools and ideas for use by the owner and his son. The main workbench has 24 drawers holding tools and small parts. Everything except power tools stores away from sanding dust, and a large drum vacuum cleaner makes cleaning easy.

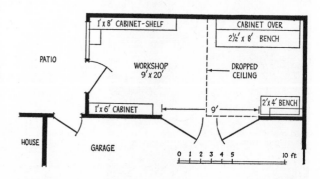

Dropped ceiling *stores lumber. Bullet lights over workbenches (son's is at right) are adjustable.*

Double doors *can be opened to garage when additional room is needed for larger projects.*

DENS & STUDIES

...for music, conversation, reading

(See coverage of this room on page 79)

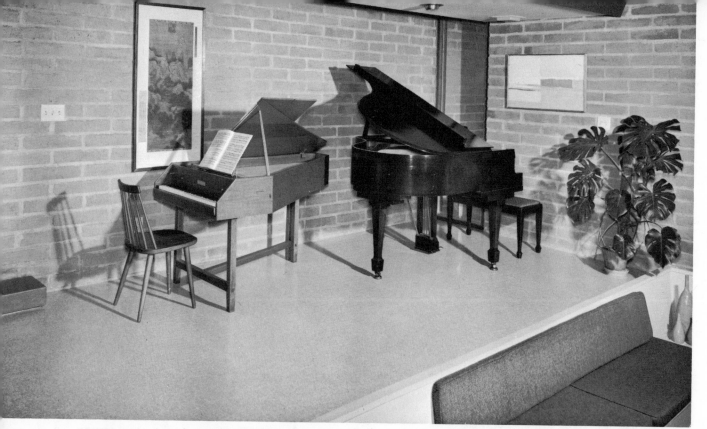

Music stage *is occupied by harpsichord and baby grand. Fixed and adjustable lights above provide adequate lighting. Walls are of burnt adobe brick. Sunken sitting area is at lower right (see photo below).*

A "stage" for home concerts

Within this room, roughly 18 by 26 feet, are three distinct activity areas—for music, for conversation, for dining. There are no structural partitions as such, but a definite feeling of separation is created by a 10 by 14-foot sitting area three steps lower than the floor grade. From this sunken area, the floor becomes in effect a stage for home concerts, and was purposely designed this way by the owners. The bedrooms and study are in a different part of the house, separated from the music area (and buffered from its sound) by an entry hall, closets, and a garden.

Built-in bench *around sunken sitting area holds pads, cushions, serves as end tables; windows overlook patio.*

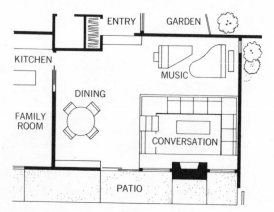

Floor plan *shows how music-dining area is separate from rest of house, has own entrance to garden.*

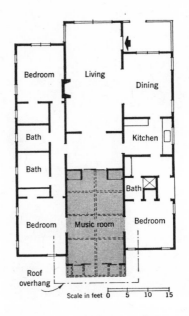

Bedroom · Living · Dining · Bath · Bath · Kitchen · Bath · Bedroom · Music room · Bedroom · Roof overhang

Scale in feet 0 5 10 15

Shaded area *is 325-square-foot music room fitted into former patio.*

New room *fills space between wings, opens to garden. Roof starts at parapet of existing flat room; overhang and trellis for sun control.*

They built a room for music

The handsome music room added to this 40-year-old house illustrates that remodeling need not be costly and extensive when space is increased without adding much exterior wall. Before the addition, the back of this typical 1920 house had two wings which defined an unused patio.

Fitted into this 325-square-foot space, the slightly pitched roof and exposed beams of the new room added new character to the house. Sliding glass doors open to the garden and extend seating room when needed.

Architect: John August Reed.

Before remodeling, *house was typical of stucco house in 1920's; this view shows two wings defining patio.*

Music room *with high ceiling adds new character to house. Paneled walls, carpet, draperies for acoustical control.*

Twice the size *of living room, new music room adds spaciousness to small house; large windows overlook garden.*

Living room ceiling *was raised and faced to match the addition; exposed beams enhance feeling of warmth.*

Big enough for a string quartet

Never underestimate how much a one-room addition may change the character of your whole house. This house was built more than 20 years ago as a simple rectangle of concrete blocks. So it remained until the owner, a musician, asked the architect to design a room where a quartet could meet to play chamber music.

The new room takes care of the music, but it also does a great deal more. Its soaring ceiling and wide expanse of glass open up the entire house. Now your view from the interior extends past the small new terrace and adjoining wild garden to a lake and distant mountains.

Architect: Winifred L. Savery.

Addition *changed former box shape of house to a more interesting L. Entrance hall was doubled in size.*

Wild garden *adjoins patio reached from music room, is viewed through large expanse of glass from living room.*

Once a porch...now a music room

A former glassed-in porch (which was too hot when the sun was shining, too cold when it was not) provided ample space for a new library-music room, studio, and dining area. Main emphasis of the remodeling was in the music room where lighter finishes and carefully planned night lighting were used. Bookcases line two walls of the new room. The third wall is glass for a spectacular view; sliding glass doors open onto a large deck. A large divider serves as the fourth wall and screens the dining area from the music room.

Architect: James Morrison Leefe.

New room *occupies space of former porch, has two walls lined with bookshelves; glass door opens onto deck.*

They wanted a stereo center

When it was first built, one of the luxury features of this subdivision house was a radiant heated patio which opened off the dining area by means of a glass wall and sliding glass door. Finding that they desired a music room more than a patio, the owners removed the partial partition between the living room and patio to open the two areas to each other completely. The floor was raised with concrete and inlaid with cork tile; the glass doors were moved to the rear. For acoustical purposes the stereophonic equipment was placed against the outside wall. The long window above the cabinets was curtained for sun protection.

Former patio *now a music room with stereo equipment against end wall so sound carries to living room.*

Ceiling beam *marks old front porch wall line. Existing fireplace, rug add to warmth and comfort.*

Remodeled for a bedroom–study

In this remodel, a new study and master bedroom share a large space created from the former living room and front porch. The living room fireplace remained to warm the new study; and its familiar comfort, along with convenient storage for games in the window seat, has made the study a favorite place for all members of the family. Two other innovations not shown in the photo above are wood storage in the near end of the window seat, and map stor-age in the wall above the mantel (with the access door near the window).

When the teacher owner has the study to himself, he has a compact work area with desk, cabinets, metal files and wall bookcase. Bedroom and study are partially sep-arated by a partition. Large sliding glass windows admit ample light, provide ventilation.

Architects: Thomas and Baar.

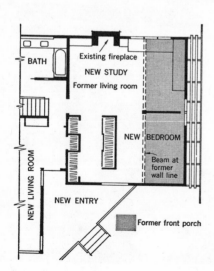

Shading *shows former front porch made part of new bed-room, study. Entry and living room were relocated.*

Clothes chest *faces new bedroom. Free-standing double closet marks off dressing space.*

Flagstone fireplace wall *has high ledge for displaying guns from collection stored in cabinet at left.*

A study with a view

This room gives the strong sense of shelter many people like in a den or study. It is just rustic enough to seem appropriate in a wooded setting overlooking a large lake, in a climate where some freezing temperatures can be expected for several months of the year.

Flagstone floor and fireplace wall, exposed posts and beams, and peeled pole ceiling do not generally suggest warmth and comfort. But Navajo rugs cover the radiant heated floor; color flickers through the uneven pole ceiling; here and there are bright pieces of Indian art; much of the furniture is built in and other pieces are solid and comfortable. One wall consists of shelves for books, hi-fi audio controls and speaker; record changer is below in a swing-out corner cabinet. Another wall contains a birch cabinet for storing a gun collection.

Architects: McFarland-Bonsall.

Double-paned windows *offer wide view. Desk is built-in; note ventilation panels below window at left.*

Bookcase wall *holds hi-fi; sliding panels open to audio controls, speaker; record changer below in cabinet.*

Study *off master bedroom has desk, reading chair, television, bookshelves; affords quiet retreat.*

Reading areas...quiet and traffic free

It takes more than books, light, and a good chair to create a really comfortable place for reading; you should look, first, for a traffic-free location, perhaps a corner of a room or a room with only one door. Furniture can often be arranged to provide a place for conversation also.

The two reading areas shown here are in the same home. The study is a quiet dead-end room; the family room corner is out of the way of traffic to the children's bedrooms.

Architects: Bissell and Duquette.

Corner of family room *with a garden view, on the quiet side of the house, invites leisurely reading; is out of traffic way to bedrooms. Magazines and books are stored on open shelves.*

Interlocking panels *are top-hung, pull out of wall recess at right to make alcove into separate room.*

An all-purpose alcove

This large alcove off the living-dining room was designed to serve as a library-den, where the family can pursue their cartographic interests. It can also serve as a guest room: For complete privacy, interlocking panels pull out of a wall recess to make the alcove into a separate room.

At one end, a built-in desk with sloping counter top holds dictionary and other reference books. A pull-out board underneath is large enough to hold large maps. Large storage shelves below are concealed by doors.

Architect: Morgan Stedman.

End wall *of alcove has sloped counter for reference books. Concealed storage shelves below hold maps and other prints. Behind flush panel doors at right, vertical compartments store leaves for dining table.*

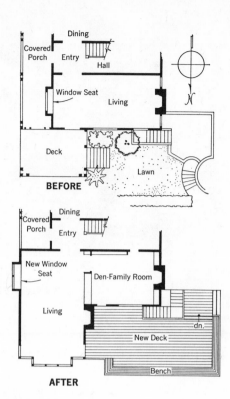

BEFORE

AFTER

Former living room fireplace *now serves new den-family room, is surrounded by bookcases with adjustable shelves.*

Family room and den are one

This mellow old house served the owner's family well for 10 years. But as the children grew up and the family's interests widened, a quiet place for reading and studying was needed.

Aside from the basement, which was dark and rather damp, there was little unused space in the house. So the architects came up with this proposal: Why not divide the present living room in two, use half as a new den-family room, and then enlarge the living room by enclosing a portion of the covered front porch and an adjoining deck. The old living room fireplace was retained and now serves the new den-family room; a second fireplace was installed for the new living room.

Architects: Liddle & Jones.

Glassed-in end *of new living room faces north for light, view beyond. New fireplace is at left.*

Old porch *is now living room; still has a window seat, but it has been moved forward (see floor plan).*

HOW-TO-DO-IT IDEAS

...if you plan to do some of the work yourself

(See techniques for installing burlap wall covering on page 95)

Lightweight steel beams *support ceiling in garage. The 2- by 4-foot acoustical softboard panels and lighting fixtures can be moved about; each fixture holds two 40-watt, rapid-start fluorescent tubes.*

Suspended ceilings: easy installation

The suspended ceiling shown on these pages was originally installed in a garage workshop; however, it could work equally well in other recreation areas — anywhere you might want to deaden sound, diffuse light, or improve appearances.

It looks like an expensive ceiling, but it's not. Generally speaking, this type of ceiling costs slightly less than a regular gypsum-board ceiling.

HOW TO INSTALL

In a typical modern garage (with trusses supporting the roof) constructing a ceiling with gypsum board or other standard material would mean adding corner blocking and 2 by 6 ceiling joists between the trusses to support panels or battens. And panels would have to be taped and painted.

A metal gridwork holds the tiles, making replacement or removal of ceiling fixtures easy. If you aren't sure just where you want ceiling lights, you can connect them to junction boxes with flexible conduit (see drawing on opposite page) and move them anywhere. This allows you to shift them around to find the best location.

Electrical outlets in the ceiling can be especially handy. They permit you to use large power tools in the middle of a garage without having to run extension cords across the floor. You mount two outlet boxes to ceiling tiles and

connect them with flexible conduit so those tiles can be relocated as desired.

Wall to wall installation is not necessary with a suspended ceiling. The one shown here stops 6 feet from the garage door, leaving an open space between the last roof truss and the door for storing sheets of plywood and long boards.

Installation can be completed in one day. First, nail prefinished right-angle metal molding to the walls about 5 inches below the bottoms of the roof trusses. Then cut the main runners or metal beams to length with tin snips, set them on the molding, and support them every 4 feet throughout their spans with pieces of No. 12 galvanized wire extending down from heavy staples in the rafters and screw eyes in the roof sheathing. These main runners are prefinished to resemble wood beams and are for appearance only; you could just as well substitute long lengths of white tees, because the wires give the strength necessary to hold the entire ceiling in position.

Next, lock the white cross tees, 4 feet long, to the main runners by bending their ends over in slots in the runners. The ceiling is now ready for the softboard tiles.

The ceiling light fixtures are designed to clamp on the metal gridwork, either to the white cross tees or the main runners. Each fixture holds two 40-watt rapid-start fluorescent tubes. You can slip a 2 by 4 foot sheet of luminous plastic paneling into place under each to enclose it and diffuse the light.

Installation: *Ceiling will cover rough trusses, rafters. Metal beams are supported by wires from rafters; steel crosspieces lock into beams.*

Space *between end of ceiling and garage doors stores pieces of lumber.*

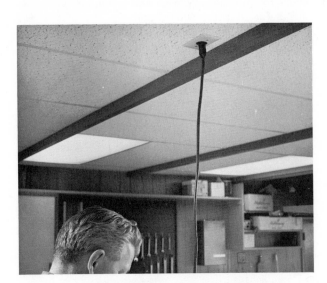

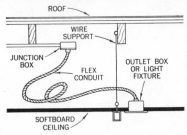

Ceiling outlets, *connected to junction boxes by flexible conduit, can be relocated by interchanging panels.*

Opaque plastic paneling *slips into place under each fluorescent light fixture, replaces softboard panels.*

Installing a resilient floor

Asphalt, vinyl, vinyl-asbestos, rubber, linoleum, and cork tiles are all excellent floor covering materials for a recreation room or recreation center. Your choice in flooring depends largely on the amount of wear and tear expected and the amount of upkeep that will be required. A wood floor, though admired for its grain and finish, is often impractical because of the likelihood of marring and scratching. Some kind of surface covering is normally recommended — not only to withstand hard wear but to help reduce noise. (The use of carpeting is discussed on page 91.)

SELECTING THE MATERIAL

On the market today there are many different types of resilient floor tiles from which to choose. Particularly suited to recreation rooms, many of the newer products feature game-board insets around which tile is laid (see photo below). Other floor tiles offer choices in wood-grain, slate, and pebble design. There are textured bamboo-design vinyl planks, vinyl sheet with photographic impressions of brick or tile, and embossed-surface vinyl and vinyl-asbestos tile and sheet materials. Also available is sheet flooring with a vinyl surface, latex cushion center layer, and felt backing. It goes over older floors without

gluing and cuts with scissors. Another new product is made of white polyester resin cast with marble or other mineral chips to make a hard, durable tile that looks like cement terrazzo. The tile is nonporous, four times harder than concrete, and is available in patterns. Still another floor covering is a new inlaid vinyl with a foam vinyl backing. It provides a cushioned surface that resists permanent indentations.

Base your decision on personal preference, the cost involved, your existing floor, and whether you are planning to do the job yourself. If the latter is true, many floor-covering shops specialize in supplies and instruction for do-it-yourself installation, and dealers are very helpful.

Only a few types of tile can withstand moisture and alkali of a concrete floor that is in direct contact with the ground. If your floor is below-grade or on-grade concrete, your choice is usually limited to asphalt or vinyl asbestos tiles. However, you may be able to use other types for an on-grade concrete floor that has a satisfactory waterproofing membrane and good drainage. Be sure to get specific advice from your dealer.

If your floor is wood, ceramic tile, or above-grade concrete (with an air space beneath), you can use asphalt, vinyl asbestos, homogeneous vinyl, linoleum, rubber, rubber plastic, or cork tiles. Ask your tile retailer about the properties of each and which one he recommends for your recreation room.

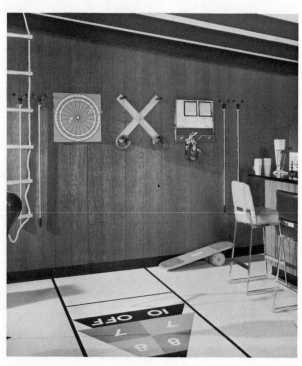

Shuffleboard inset *can be incorporated in vinyl-asbestos floor by using tiles with special design.*

Durable floor *for dancing has large record inset; contributes to overall decorative scheme for teen-agers.*

Once you have selected the tile, there are three further steps: determining the quantity, preparing the subfloor, and laying the tile.

HOW MANY TILES ARE NEEDED?

To figure the number of tiles needed, measure the length and width of the room in inches; divide each of these figures by the width of the tile (usually 6 or 9 inches); increase any fraction to the nearest whole number; multiply one resulting figure by the other. This gives the number of tiles needed for a rectangular room; figure separately each offset section in an irregular room. It's a good idea to add 2 or 4 percent for wastage.

TOOLS AND SUPPLIES

For most types of tiles you will need an adhesive spreader (toothed strip of metal or cardboard about 5 by 12 inches), a linoleum knife or tile cutter, a chalkline, a linoleum roller, yardstick, and carpenter's square. (Most floor covering stores rent tile cutters and linoleum rollers for a nominal fee.)

For old floors (and some new ones) you will need a floor sander. This also can be rented. If you have to remove old tile before retiling, you'll want a scraper and a blowtorch.

Other supplies will depend on the kind of floor and tile. Wood floors require a layer of plywood, masonite or particle board, a crack filler (a powder to be mixed with water), and an adhesive. For concrete floors you will need a floor primer and an adhesive. *Be sure to get the adhesive recommended for the tile you are buying.*

PREPARING THE FLOOR

First, and most important, allow plenty of time for preparing the floor and laying the tile. You may find that even a small room with no apparent irregularities may take a whole day. Clear the room of furniture and other objects and remove the baseboard moulding.

Irregularities in the floor will give an uneven tile surface. It's important, therefore, to tighten all the loose floor boards and to prepare a very smooth surface. To insure a good bond between tile and floor, completely remove all material such as wax, paint, or varnish, as well as oil or grease spots.

If Your Floor Is Wood

Make sure all floor boards are tight and all nails set. Plane ridges if necessary. Fill cracks or slight hollows with crack filler. Sand thoroughly.

If the floor is too rough to prepare properly, or if there is no subfloor, you will need to cover it with a layer of plywood, masonite, or particle board, sold at lumber yards in special grades for this purpose. These should be nailed with cement-coated, galvanized, or screw nails to prevent "pop-up." Start nailing from one corner or in the center of a panel; nailing the four corners first can make the panel springy.

If Your Floor Is Concrete

If the concrete has been finished with wax, paint, or any other substance, sand it thoroughly. After the floor is clean, apply a coat of primer of the type recommended for the tile you use. Scrub the primer well into the concrete. A large, round Tampico fiber brush, such as a dairy brush, is good for this. A wide paint brush may be used at the edges of the floor. Primer must dry for several hours, until all solvent odor has disappeared. *Do not walk on the floor until it's dry.* No lining is used with concrete.

If Your Floor Has Been Previously Tiled

You can lay new tile over the old tile if the old tile is in quite good condition. However, some experts recommend removing old tile. Be sure to remove all wax before starting, and do not put new joints directly over joints in the old tile.

If old tile flooring is not in good condition, you will need to remove it. First, pull up all the old tile. Remove old adhesive with a scraper and a blowtorch. After scraping off as much of the heat-softened mastic as possible, sand with coarse sandpaper.

A filler used to "float the floor" is now being recommended for use on old ceramic tile. It seals all irregularities and cracks and eliminates the need for sanding. (See your dealer for specific instructions.)

HOW TO LAY THE NEW FLOOR

When you are satisfied with the condition of the subfloor — all the wax, grease, and dirt removed and the cracks and holes filled — you are now ready to begin laying tiles.

1. Make guide lines by finding the center points of the side walls; connect these two points with a chalk line down the middle of the room. Repeat for the end walls. Check the crossed lines with a carpenter's square.

2. Along the chalk lines, lay a neat row of uncemented tile from the center point to one side wall, another to an end wall. Measure the distance between the wall and the last tile. If the distance is less than 2 inches or more than 8 inches, move the center line 4½ inches closer to the wall.

3. If you are using a quick-setting adhesive, spread enough at a time for about 15 tiles. With slow-setting adhesive, spread an entire quarter section or more at once and allow it to become tacky before placing the tiles. Be careful not to cover the guide lines with adhesive. Spread it smooth and not too thick.

4. Set the tiles in place; don't slide them, or you'll push the adhesive up between them. Any that gets on the tile surface should be wiped off immediately with a damp cloth. If a spot of adhesive should dry on the tile, remove it with fine steel wool and soapy water. Press each tile down firmly with your hand, especially at the edges. Lay all whole tiles first, leaving until last those that must be cut to fit the edges. The diagram on the next page shows an easy way to measure for custom-fitting edges.

Asphalt tile can be cut more easily if you heat the back of the tile with a blowtorch to soften it. Then cut

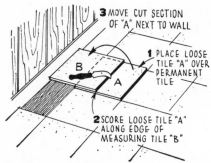

A simple way *to fit tile at the edge of a room.*

with tile cutter or tin snips. Or you can score an unheated tile several times with a linoleum knife and snap in two. Other kinds of tiles can be cut with a tile cutter, knife, or scissors without heating. If the tile ends in a doorway, lay the tile halfway through (to end under a door, where possible). Then finish the edge with a metal strip (over wood floors) or a beveled asphalt strip (over concrete). Purchase the strip where you buy the tile.

5. To fit around pipes or other obstructions in a room, first make a paper pattern to fit the space exactly. Then trace the outline onto the tile and cut with scissors.

6. To complete the floor installation, you may want to use vinyl coving around the edges of the room, particularly under cabinets or other storage areas. Vinyl cove base is available in a variety of colors styled to complement any decorating scheme. After cutting the proper lengths to fit into place, apply the adhesive to the back of the coving and press it against the wall. (Your dealer will help you with specific details.)

If you are laying rubber, linoleum, or cork tiles, you will need to roll the floor afterwards. For a large room, you'll need a linoleum roller.

Don't roll asphalt or vinyl asbestos tile. If the edges of asphalt tile appear raised, room warmth will flatten them in a few days.

Let the floor dry thoroughly, at least overnight; then clean it (and wax or polish, if desired) before you move any furniture into the room. Do not mop the tiles for at least a week.

Establish guide *lines by finding center points of opposite walls, connecting points with chalk lines.*

Place row *of uncemented tile along chalk lines from center point to one side wall, another to end wall.*

Spread adhesive *smoothly, don't cover guide lines. Allow to become tacky before placing tiles.*

Set tiles *in place without sliding them. Butt each tile against adjoining tiles; remove excess adhesive.*

Trace patterns *of pipe or other obstructions on paper, trace outline onto tile, cut with scissors.*

Complete *floor installation with vinyl coving. Cut pieces to proper lengths and fit into place.*

Carpeting for heavy traffic

It is a well-known fact that carpeting contributes greatly in the never-ending search for ways to counteract noise. In a recreation room, carpeting is a good answer. It deadens air-borne sound and softens the impact of footsteps or objects falling or scraping on the floor. Sound-absorption tests have established that there is a definite noise reduction coefficient for various carpets. However, even with these figures most people are reluctant to make such an investment for a recreation room. What, then, is the answer?

"OUTDOOR" CARPETING INDOORS

Introduced on the market as a covering for patios and decks or to define outdoor sitting and dining areas, an ever-increasing percentage of this felted carpeting now being sold is being used indoors; in family rooms, game rooms, utility areas — wherever the situation calls for a carpet that will take lots of abuse. Although it does not absorb noise quite as well as regular carpeting, this synthetic material does reduce it.

In addition to withstanding wear and tear, outdoor carpeting provides color, a non-skid surface, and attractive texture. Because its fibers absorb very little moisture, it resists most stains. It is fairly resilient, although the fibers will mat down in heavy traffic areas.

The Pioneer: Polypropylene

Most outdoor carpeting is composed of inert, synthetic fibers. These fibers can be needlepunched, tufted, or knitted on a carpet machine to produce felted or pile finishes. Since dye is put into the basic solution from which the fibers are produced, the carpeting is highly resistant to fading from sunlight.

The longest established and still best-selling type of synthetic outdoor carpeting is made of a fiber called polypropylene olefin, with a backing of resistant synthetic resin. In appearance, such carpets resemble pressed felt. They are available in various widths and colors. Some are embossed into brick, pebble, or tile patterns to give a slight three-dimensional effect.

Although highly resistant to wear, it's not recommended for use on stairs. Elsewhere, the subflooring should be as smooth as possible.

Polypropylene Variations

The same fiber is being used in some cut pile and some random-textured carpeting (a combination of cut and uncut loops, also called tip-sheared carpeting). Depending on how it's made, very different effects can be achieved. Some manufacturers make fringed area rugs out of this carpeting.

One product uses polypropylene rubber fiber with a slight sheen, in a random-textured face. This material is tufted into a sheet of polypropylene and backed with a non-skid synthetic rubber in an embossed grid design.

Acrylic, Nylon, Vinyl

Also in the field of indoor-outdoor carpeting are the solution-dyed acrylic fibers. They are available in tweedy mixtures, a tightly looped pile and a random-textured pile. Another type of carpeting is a 100 percent nylon fiber on a synthetic rubber backing with a plush cut pile. A solid vinyl carpeting with a mosaic pattern or tweed effect is also available. This type has excellent resistance to staining, but is not as soft underfoot as other outdoor-carpeting materials.

INSTALLATION AND MAINTENANCE

You can lay outdoor carpeting yourself. You cut it with scissors or a sharp knife, and install it in one of three ways:

1. Laid loosely.
2. Attached around the edges with a double-faced tape.
3. Secured with an adhesive.

A word of caution: The use of adhesive may cause problems if you ever wish to remove the whole carpet for replacement. However, small pieces can usually be lifted with little trouble.

Regular Cleaning Is Necessary

Indoor-outdoor carpeting should be given a regular cleaning just like carpeting used in other parts of the house. Most types can be washed with warm water and a mild detergent. In between times, you can wipe up most household products that might have been spilled on the surface with a damp sponge.

Protect Against Fire Damage

All synthetic materials have a relatively low melting point, so take special care to prevent and protect your carpeting from fire damage — as from cigarettes or fireplace sparks. If you have to, you can repair burns or holes by cutting out the damaged sections and replacing them with new material.

Check springiness *by pressing brush against hand. Good bristles spread evenly, feel silky, are straight.*

Part bristles *and look for inner plug; if more than half the size of base, the brush is inferior.*

Examine bristle ends *to see if most are "flagged" (divided); flagged nylon should look like this.*

Basic three: *angled sash brush for trim, medium brush for small areas, and large wall brush.*

How skillful is your painting?

It used to be that the easy part of painting a room was to select the paint and the hard part was to put it on the walls. The new paints of today have changed this concept. Whether you use a brush, roller, or spray gun, most paints are relatively easy to apply.

Most people who own their own home acquire some skill at painting, but forget or have never learned many of the things a professional painter does automatically. Here are some tips from the professionals that can make the painting of your recreation room easier.

CHOOSING THE RIGHT PAINT BRUSH

Your choice of a paint brush depends partly on what paint or other finish you'll be using.

Nylon brushes are considered best for use with water-base paints (latexes, including synthetic rubber, PVA, acrylic, and vinyl). Good nylon filaments wear exceptionally well, do not absorb water, and are not affected by alkalinity.

Hog-bristle brushes are the traditional choice for use with oil-base paints, enamels, alkyds, varnishes, lacquers, epoxy paints, stains and metal primers. Though hog bristles are not nearly as long-lasting as nylon, most painters

feel they have superior brushing qualities. But even for some oil-base finishes, nylon is gaining in favor.

For lacquer or shellac, choose only a bristle brush, since the solvents in these finishes tend to soften nylon.

HOW TO USE A BRUSH

When painting with a brush, dip only about a third of the bristle into the paint. If you take more, paint will load up in the heel and run down the handle. After dipping, most experts slap the brush gently against the side of the can to remove excess paint. You also can drag it lightly against the rim, although this is slower.

When using a quick-drying, water-mixed paint, first dip your brush in water and squeeze it out, and then start painting. The water helps prevent paint from getting into the heel of the brush and quickly hardening there.

For enamel work, you should flow on the enamel generously with less pressure than with flat paints. If you brush it out too much, the finish is bumpy. Try to cover a small area at a time, then level it off by brushing crosswise. Work quickly and never go back to touch up a tacky spot.

You can almost always apply enamel more smoothly with a brush; but on large surfaces such as a kitchen wall you can speed the job considerably by using a roller to lay on the enamel and then using a brush to "feather" it out. Lay on about a 2-foot-wide strip with the roller, then smooth it out with the brush. Roll the next strip about 8 inches away from the first and work over with the brush to join the two.

When painting edged objects, such as shelves, you'll avoid dribbling if you brush out to the edge, rather than in from the edge. Similarly, let your brush strokes end at a groove or other indentation, rather than drag across it and "load" with paint.

When painting trim, keep a clean brush at hand for dusting just before you paint. On window frames, "cutting in" with a brush (painting right up to the line) without masking off the glass is difficult for a beginner. You can use masking tape, or try a method the experts sometimes employ when they need to mask: Cut 2-inch-wide strips from the smooth, unserrated edges of newspaper. Roll up these strips, soak the roll in water, shake it out, and mask one or two windows at a time with some of these strips. Wipe the frames to remove any drops of water, and paint. Remove the strips when the painting is completed. The newsprint adheres well when wet, but will fall off when dry.

IF YOU USE A ROLLER

You should work slowly and smoothly with a roller (it will cover the area rapidly, regardless). Quick strokes result in spatters and uneven pressure makes bubbles. You need not roll uniformly in one direction. In fact, the job will be better if you roll every which way.

Painters recommend that when applying flat wall paints with a roller you start each new strip a foot or two away and work back toward the wet edge of the last strip, lapping into it halfway. The resulting coat is much more even.

WHERE TO START

Where you start painting can make considerable difference in the results. If you're ambitiously redoing the whole room, it is fairly obvious that you should start with the ceiling. But you should also start in a corner; and whether you're using a brush or a roller, you should start by painting a strip about 2 feet wide completely across the ceiling the shorter way. You will be returning sooner on the next strip, and so there will be less likelihood of lap marks. Paint each strip only as wide as you can reach comfortably (never more than 3 feet wide).

Again to prevent lap marks, paint the entire ceiling without stopping and as rapidly as you can.

Next, paint the walls, which are easier. Simply start at a corner and continue around the room. Then comes the baseboard and window trim. Paint the doors last.

Wherever possible, start at the top and work down, whether you're painting a wall, a chair, or a boat. You will have fewer runs and spatters on fresh paint.

Start refinishing a door by painting the frame. Then paint the door's edges and on each immediately wipe off with a rag any overlapping edge of wet paint on the door faces. If it's a flush door, paint the faces. If it's a paneled door, paint the panels and their moldings, again wiping off any overlap. Then paint the horizontal rails, and finish with the vertical stiles. (You may see a professional just start in at the top of a door and paint everything on the way down. He can do this because he can apply paint fast enough so that he's always lapping into fresh wet paint.)

SPRAY CANS — A SPECIAL TECHNIQUE

Pressure spray paint cans have been with us for quite a few years and by now you can find ones that contain paints and clear finishes for both indoor and outdoor use, flat as well as glossy enamels, and almost any color you desire.

Most produce good durable finishes. They usually cover small jobs neatly and much more easily than a brush does, and are also handy for such larger jobs as refinishing wicker or metal furniture.

Although you can obtain excellent results with a spray can one time, you may have a miserable time the next. Here are the major reasons why results can vary so much, and some suggestions on how you can be more assured of success:

Temperature. Aerosol spray cans are designed to be used at ordinary room temperature — around 70°. If you just grab a spray can from a shelf in a cold garage and use it immediately, the resulting paint film may sag, run, or form bubbles. You should submerge a cold can in warm water (not over 90°) for about 5 minutes, or leave it in a heated room for a few hours before using it.

Technique. The way you spray can make a great difference, particularly on a smooth surface. Whenever possible, arrange the job so the surface to be sprayed lies flat. Then shake the can vigorously for at least 30 seconds (or longer, if the directions on it so advise). Hold the can about 14 to 18 inches away from the surface you're painting, and use light "dusting" strokes, passing completely across and beyond the surface, depressing and releasing the spray head at the beginning and end of each stroke. This gives you a thin mist coat. Two or more such coats are better than one heavy coat and much less likely to sag.

Avoid stopping and reversing a stroke on the work — you will likely get a heavy buildup of paint where you stop. If a thin paint film sags or runs, the can is either too cold, as already mentioned, or you are holding it too close to the work. If the paint film is rough-textured, the can is too warm or you are holding it too far away from the work. You should always press the head down completely to insure a uniform spray.

Clogging. If the spray-head doesn't spray, or sprays and then sputters and clogs, first try turning it to right and left a few times. That often clears it. If not, remove the spray-head (simply pull it up off the can) and clean it out with a toothpick or fine wire, or soak it in lacquer thinner. Push the cleaned head back onto the can (holding a finger over its face to prevent spraying), and give it a half-turn to seat it. If it is still clogged, you can purchase a replacement spray-head at a paint store.

Wall coverings for wear and tear

Vinyl and burlap wall coverings can be an unusually effective alternative to the painted or wall-papered plaster-board wall in your newly acquired recreation room. Both of these materials are easy to install and maintain, and they are durable. Either can be an answer whether you are trying to hide the imperfections of an old wall or looking for a different approach for a new room. Advantages of both, along with instructions for installation, are discussed below and on the next two pages.

VINYL WALL COVERINGS

Vinyl wall coverings first appeared on the market about 1946; at that time the choice of patterns was limited, the materials were designed primarily for commercial uses, and installation was expensive. Today, vinyl wall coverings are frequently used in new, remodeled, or re-decorated houses to simulate wood, reed, stone, leather, and a wide variety of fabrics from moire taffetas to burlap. And prices are such that everyone can use vinyl.

Durable and virtually grease-proof, vinyl is especially useful for recreation rooms where wall surfaces are apt to get marked and scuffed.

Washable wall papers have a thin protective coat of plastic or latex to help prevent them from soiling; you sponge off surface dirt and finger prints with soap and water. The vinyls, however, are almost impervious to grease, wax, and other household substances likely to stain or spot, and they can actually be scrubbed — even cleaned with a mild abrasive if necessary.

How They Are Made

Sheets of vinyl plastic are laminated to a backing material — such as woven or pressed-fiber fabric, paper, or fiber-glass — and embossed with textures or printed with designs. Because the background color is an integral part of the vinyl, fading is slight. In the lightweight vinyls you find predominantly light colors and a majority of the prints; in the heavier vinyls you find the deeper colors and a wide range of textures.

Also available is vinyl-covered wall paneling. Most lumberyards carry both gypsum-board and plywood, surfaced with plastic in realistic wood tones, dull and textured finishes, and soft pastel colors. Latest among such materials are pre-finished fir and Philippine mahogany plywood with a grained vinyl facing to protect from scuffing, dirt, and staining.

Where to Buy Them

Lightweight vinyls are displayed like wallpaper: Dealers have sample books or sample strips of material, usually available for you to borrow.

The lightweight vinyls come in wallpaper-size rolls, 24 to 27 inches wide. A standard roll contains 36 square feet of material, enough to cover 30 square feet of wall allowing for trim and matching patterns. The heavier vinyls come in 18 to 54-inch widths and are sold by the yard.

When buying wallpaper, you must often take a minimum of two or three rolls; vinyl wall coverings, however, can be purchased in single rolls.

How to Hang Them

The vinyls can be applied to any smooth, clean background that would normally take paper or paint. Be sure to tell your dealer where you plan to put the vinyl and get his advice about preparing the background. Each manufacturer of a vinyl wall covering recommends a special adhesive for his material, and it's best to use it.

In one respect the vinyls are easier to hang than regular wallpaper, because they won't tear as easily. If you have to make a joint, however, they won't stretch, contract, or slide as easily. Seams are butted rather than overlapped. Excess adhesive should be wiped off with a damp sponge before it dries (it can etch the surface of the vinyl if it remains too long). Vinyl-covered wall panelings can be installed either with nails or an adhesive recommended by the manufacturer.

How to Clean Them

Most common stains and scuff marks can be removed with soap or detergent and water. If this is unsuccessful, you can try a stronger detergent, or diluted household bleach or ammonia. Some stains will respond to household cleaning fluids. Stronger solvents such as paint thinner should be tested first for their effect on the vinyl. Acetone should not be used because it will soften the vinyl. A mild abrasive can be used when other means fail. *However, it is wise to consult the manufacturer or retailer before trying to clean a particularly difficult or hard-to-remove stain.*

How to Remove Them

Though vinyl wall covering will last for many years, you may want to redecorate long before it wears out. It can be re-covered or painted over, providing it is adhering well to the wall. Many dealers and manufacturers recommend that vinyls be removed. But remember that the adhesives are strong: take care not to remove any wall surface at the same time.

The fabric-backed vinyls are best removed by slitting each panel with a razor blade into 4- to 6-inch strips, loosening the top edge and pulling the strip straight down.

Spots, *greasy fingerprints can be scrubbed off vinyl.*

Vinyl overlaid *plywood wall withstands wear and tear.*

The paper-backed vinyls can be removed in either of two ways: sand the vinyl down to the paper backing, then apply steam to loosen the paper from the wall; or separate the vinyl from the paper, starting at one corner of the strip. The vinyl should come off in one sheet and the paper can be removed with steam.

To paint or re-cover a smooth-surfaced vinyl, you must size the wall beforehand. Either a water base paint or vinyl paint can be used.

BURLAP: FOR A PROBLEM WALL

Burlap makes a handsome and durable fabric for covering walls. This is especially true if you are remodeling to gain a recreation room. It hides cracks, patches, and blotchy color, and has enough give to take shifting and movement in a house without cracking or peeling. Burlap also helps to dampen sound. In some people's opinion, it is simpler to hang than wallpaper. You paste only one surface instead of two, and you hang the burlap in a strip from the top instead of folding as you do wallpaper. It doesn't tear, and if you make a mistake, it's easy and inexpensive to rectify.

Where to Buy

Buy your burlap through a yardage store. In a medium weight, 40 to 50 inches wide, it sells for quite a bit less than $1.00 a yard; in a heavy weight, sometimes 55 inches wide, it costs a little more. You should use at least medium weight to conceal any wall color. If you buy colored burlap, be sure to get enough for the entire job. You may find that dye lot colors vary and a week after you've bought burlap of a certain color you won't be able to duplicate it exactly.

Supplies You Will Need

You will need wall sizing and a brush; fabric paste and a large brush for applying it; drafting tape (less sticky than masking tape and easier to remove; it's available at stationery and art stores); a steel measuring tape, sharp scissors, a short-nap paint roller, and a plasterer's trowel.

Prepare the Walls First

To prepare the walls of the room, fill any deep cracks or holes with spackle or crack filler, and sand the patches smooth. It facilitates the job to remove top molding (but not baseboards). On textured walls, prepare the surface by sanding it smooth or hanging blank stock (available at paint and wallpaper stores); size all new plaster walls or old painted walls to reduce their porosity, then paint the woodwork.

Preparing and Cutting the Burlap

Unroll the burlap, clip the selvage at one end about 1 inch below the cut line, and pull a cross thread. Cut across the resulting line to get a true cross grain. From this cut edge, measure off your lengths, adding an inch or two to allow some leeway. To be sure of measuring from a true cross grain, clip the selvage at the end of each panel and pull a cross thread before cutting the fabric. Press out any creases with a steam iron.

When the panels are cut to the right length, you'll need

to trim off the selvage. Pull a lengthwise thread just along the selvage for the full length of the panel, and cut on the resulting line. If you use drafting tape to keep the edges from fraying, apply it along the gap left by the pulled thread before you cut the selvage.

Begin by dropping a plumb line about a foot away from a corner. (Do not attempt a corner joint; walls may have settled out of plumb.) Start on an inconspicuous wall to get the feel of burlap.

Brush or roll paste evenly on the wall, covering the area that will be underneath the first panel.

Hanging the Panels

Hang the first panel, butting the edge to the plumb line. Press the burlap against the wall with your hands, smoothing it straight across the top, then pressing it against the wall at the center, working out to the sides. Then go over the entire panel with a roller or trowel (see photo on page 85). To fit the fabric top and bottom, crease each edge with the trowel or the pointed end of the scissors, lift it slightly, and cut the edge along the crease. Replace the burlap and flatten it with the trowel.

Continue this procedure around the room, butting each panel against the previous one. The burlap may stretch a bit as you press it on the wall. If it does, drop a new plumb line and trim off the excess burlap with a sharp razor blade before hanging the next panel.

Remove any tape before the paste dries. Gently pull it off with one hand as you smooth the fibers in place with the other. Trowel or roll the butted joint.

If you ever want to change the color of your walls, you can always paint over burlap.

Pull cross thread, *cut lengths along pulled thread for true cross grain. To prevent fraying, press drafting tape along cutting line next to pulled thread gap.*

Burlapped walls *were a family project in this family TV room-studio; they deaden sound, are durable.*